READY TO SELL YOUR FARM?

ADRIAN SPITTERS FCSI, CFP, FMA
SENIOR WEALTH ADVISOR

Heart Beat
PRODUCTIONS

READY TO SELL YOUR FARM?

or

Transfer it to the Next Generation

ISBN: 978-1-895112-4-81

Published by
HeartBeat Productions Inc.
Box 633 Abbotsford, BC Canada V2T 6Z8
email: info@heartbeat1.com
604.852.3761

Edited by Dr. Win Wachsmann
Cover design, artwork: Dr. Carrie Wachsmann
Cover Photo: Sutiporn Somnam © 123RF.com

Printed in USA

Heart Beat PRODUCTIONS

THIS BOOK IS DEDICATED
TO FARMERS
WHO DON'T
WANT TO WORK FOREVER

TABLE OF CONTENTS

To farmers who don't want to work forever

One day your farm will change hands...

Will you transfer your farm to your children,

extended family, or sell to a third party?

Will it be on your terms?

CHAPTER 1

INTRODUCTION

Most farmers don't have time to think too far ahead into the future. That's because they're busy attending to the needs of today: producing high-quality products, overseeing employees, and managing the mind-boggling number of details that go into owning a farm.

If they *do* think about the future, it's usually in terms of new government regulations, availability and price of land or quota for future expansion, or even what the weather will be like

The truly long-term decisions, like when to sell or transition your farm (not to mention how to do it), are mentally filed away under the heading, "Bridges to cross when I've come to it."

But that bridge may be a lot closer than you think.

No time to deal with the issue

Understandably, most farmers have great difficulty in setting aside the time to plan for the future of their farm business in addition to working on their farm.

To quote John F. Kennedy, *"The time to mend the roof is when the sun is shining."*

It is the planning for the future of your farm while the sun is shining that will help protect your farm, and ultimately your family, from the rainstorms that loom ahead.

You see, recently conducted surveys[1] of privately-owned family businesses, including farms across North America, report that approximately 40% of business owners expect to exit their family business in the next five years. That number goes up to a whopping 70% within the next ten years.

---

[1] *The information from these surveys was derived from various sources, including Deloitte, PWC, Laird, Tyne, CFIB and MassMutual.*

These statistics are a direct result of the fact that baby-boomers are nearing retirement.

A significant number of these business owners indicate that they will be relying on the ongoing success of their business to finance their future lifestyle – either by selling the business, or from collecting a salary or dividend after they exit day-to-day management.

All this applies to farmers like you.

So, ask yourself:

1. Do you have a plan in place to increase the value of your farm before it's time to sell?
2. Do you have a plan in place that will enable you to transfer your farm to your family or sell to a third party?
3. Have you planned how to retire on your terms, instead of being forced to transfer or sell your farm on someone else's?
4. Are you proactively preparing a successor who will enable the continuity of your farm operation?

Or are you one of the 65% of business owners who haven't planned that far ahead?[2]

---

[2] http://www.bdo.ca/en/Services/Advisory/Business-Transition/pages/The-BDO-SuccessCare-Program.aspx

It's true: most farmers haven't planned for the day when they will transition or sell their farm. That makes them vulnerable to an **involuntary sale**, meaning they will be forced to sell their farm due to death, disability, or other reasons.

As you can see, the question of when and how to transition your farm is something that needs to be answered sooner rather than later.

The first step is to have a plan. Having a plan in place *now* can save you untold time and trouble in the future…and it can also help ensure that when the time *does* come to transition your farm, you do it *right*.

The stakes are high. For an overwhelming number of farmers, the sale of their farm will be their primary source of income for retirement.

That's why it's crucial that they get it right. Otherwise, they will deny themselves the chance at much-needed income during a time when every dollar counts.

For others, their major goal is to keep their farm in the family. But transitioning your farm, even to your own children, is a long and complex process.

Finally, *everyone* wants to cement their legacy and good name long after the transaction takes place.

I know that farmers are also **business owners**... your business is one of the most important in the entire world. I understand that owning a farm isn't easy. Yet I also know that the decision to one-day sell or transfer out of your farm can be just as difficult.

My name is Adrian Spitters. I'm a Senior Wealth Advisor with Assante Capital Management Ltd. As the child of a farmer, I can appreciate the hard work you've put into establishing a successful farm.

I've prepared this special book just for you. In just a few short pages, we'll look at some of the challenges facing farmers who want to quit working someday, what the most successful farmers are doing now, and where you can get additional help.

One of my goals is to give you ideas on how to plan for *your* eventual transition into retirement and have peace of mind.

CHAPTER 2

THE CHALLENGES FACING FARMERS WHO WANT TO QUIT WORK SOMEDAY

Here are two plain and simple truths.

The **first** is that no matter how much you enjoy what you do, you probably don't want to do it forever.

At some point in our lives, we all want to wind down, explore other interests, and just generally live life at a slower pace. It's called retirement.

The **second** truth is that retirement is becoming increasingly difficult and expensive. This is especially true for farmers like you.

There are unique challenges you face that must be overcome in order for you to sell or transition your farm and retire the way you've always dreamed.

Some Challenges You Will Face:

1. How to determine the value of your farm
2. Where and how to find the right buyer
3. How to choose the right time to sell
4. Deciding whether to transition your farm to a family member or sell to a non-related party
5. Determining whether selling your farm will bring in enough proceeds to fund your retirement and other financial goals
6. Ensuring the orderly payment and transition of ownership/management of your farm to your successor/heir
7. How to minimize the taxes that come from selling your farm
8. Ensuring you have sufficient assets to secure you and your family's future

And the biggest Challenge?

You don't want to think about leaving

Underlying many of the reasons for failing to address the inevitable transition of their farm is the fear farmers have of leaving what they have worked so hard to build. The farm is their life and they do not want to give up control.

We can show you how you can gradually delegate control while finding a way to still employ your unique abilities. You can develop a track that will allow you to slowly step away from the farm while doing what is needed to protect your family and the farm.

And what about Conflicts with Family/Employees?

It's amazing how often family dynamics become almost insurmountable when thinking about transitioning your farm.

One or more of your children may be working in your farm while others have left the rural life behind. In family gatherings, the discussion will rarely move in that direction.

However, everyone is giving it some thought. And that applies to your children and their spouses as well. You love them all dearly but they will have different expectations of what the transition should look like.

As a result, many farmers are reluctant to attempt

reconciling the differing personalities, values and expectations that exist in their family unit.

Who wants to start a family argument over the Thanksgiving or Christmas turkey?

By now you know your hot buttons and those of your family members. So, the easiest thing is to bite your lip or walk out of the room if that can be done circumspectly.

So, you may try to defer the decisions and discussions, but there comes a time when all these issues will need to be addressed.

With the appropriate structures in place, you can address any potential conflict in advance and prepare the way to move ahead with a transition plan.

But it's Still A few Years Off

Now you may be thinking, "Retirement is still a few years off. Why do I have to think about this now?"

The answer is that by thinking and planning *now*, you can drastically improve your chances of retiring how you want to in the future. That's because, when it comes to selling your farm, you can either do it **by choice** or **by necessity**.

To sell by necessity means that you really have no other option than to sell your farm, often as quickly as possible, to the highest bidder (who may be looking at the stresses you face and as a result will not be offering fair market value at all). Poor health, bankruptcy, or even a dramatic change in the industry may force your hand to sell.

The main problem with selling by necessity is that you often have to settle for a lower price. A secondary problem is that once your farm is sold, you will suddenly find yourself without a livelihood, and with no idea whether you have enough money on which to retire.

Selling by choice, on the other hand, means that *you* choose the timing and terms of your sale. *You* get to decide who you sell to and for how much.

Best of all, you can coordinate your sale within an overall retirement plan, factoring in your investments, taxes, and other financial goals.

The result?

The knowledge that you can retire, stay retired, and make retirement everything you want it to be.

CHAPTER 3

THE NEED FOR A PLAN

There's one thing that separates a farmer who sells voluntarily from those who sell by necessity: the former has a transition plan.

No matter how young or old you are, you need to have a plan. Saying "It's too early" is like saying, "I don't need to put my seatbelt on yet, I just pulled out of the garage. I'll wait until I'm on the highway."

The fact is, it's ***never*** too early. The sooner you have a plan, the sooner you can more ably avoid the unexpected bumps that every business owner faces at some point or another.

General Dwight Eisenhower, former president of the United States, said it this way:

"Failing to plan is planning to fail."

The Basics of a Good Transition Plan

Remember that a *plan* is a series of steps, determined in advance, designed to help you reach a specific objective.

The word "objective" is especially important. After all, you can't know what steps to take until you first know where you want to go.

What might a transition/succession plan include?

The formal succession plan includes information about matters such as:

1. The identity of the successor or successors;
2. How the successor will be trained for his or her role;
3. The roles of other key managers during the transition;
4. The mechanics for the purchase or sale of shares in the farm;
5. The distribution of ownership;
6. Taxation and legal considerations;
7. Financial considerations;
8. Retirement considerations;

9. A procedure for monitoring the process and dealing with disputes and problems; and

10. A timetable.

So, what might a transition plan look like?

I would like to suggest the following guideline for a farm transition plan. In the following chapters, we will look at each one of these eight components.

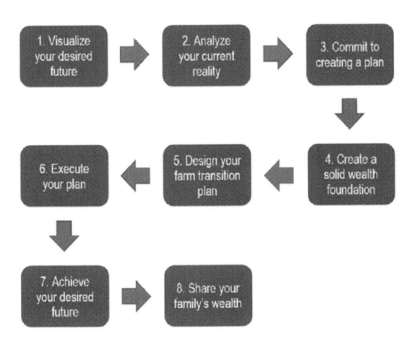

Please understand that this will not be an exhaustive discussion. For detailed steps and a wide range of planning documents, please contact the author. As a skilled advisor, I have a extensive resources available to assist you to make the best decisions possible.

This book is an introduction to the farm transition process - a task that may take several months and many conversations with family members and advisors.

CHAPTER 4

STEP 1:
VISUALIZE YOUR DESIRED FUTURE

1. Visualize your desired future

The first thing your transition plan should contain, then, is a **vision** of your desired future. A **vision** is a vivid picture of your future based on your goals, dreams and desires. Having a vision helps to clarify what is a priority for your life.

Remember, it's hard to get lost if you know where you are going.

Here is a sampling of the many questions that can be addressed. Feel free to add to the list.

1. What are your core values and principles?
2. Why do you continue to operate your farm ?

3. What do you want to accomplish in your life?
4. What dreams do you have for yourself and your family?
5. What legacy would you like to leave?
6. Will you stay on the farm and continue in some fashion?
7. When (if ever) will you be ready for a change in lifestyle?
8. Have you discussed the above questions with your spouse?
9. Does your vision of retirement match up with your spouse's?
10. Have you discussed passing your farm to your farming child(ren) while balancing non-farming child(ren)'s interests?

I'm sure you can think of more questions to ponder.

Sometimes it is helpful to meet with a Wealth Advisor who will take the time to get to know your true fears, challenges, advantages, excitements, opportunities, lifetime goals and aspirations for you, your family, farm, and legacy.

Telling a stranger about your aspirations isn't easy. However, if you think of your advisor as a valued confidant who will help you plan and achieve your vision, the process becomes less scary.

Their role is to help you visualize what your future could hold, and then create a summary report outlining the steps you should take to achieve it.

You will find a sample **Farm Wealth Planning Checklist** – Chapter 21

CHAPTER 5

STEP 2:
ANALYZE YOUR CURRENT REALITY

An effective transition plan should include a thorough analysis of what I like to call your **current reality**.

> 2. Analyze your current reality

This step involves exploring all areas of your personal, family and farm life that can have a financial impact on your wealth.

Think of it as an inventory of what you have to work with.

1. What is your current income?
2. What kind of expenses do you have?

3. What assets do you have? Real estate, stocks and bonds, RRSP's? Are you minimizing personal taxes on these non-farm assets?

4. What kind of liabilities do you have? Short term, long term?

5. How is your current health? What does your future hold?

6. Are you maximizing income splitting opportunities with family members?

7. Are you farming as a proprietor, partnership or corporation? Do you know how to minimize tax exposure on your farming income in each scenario?

8. If you run your farm as a proprietor, do you understand how incorporation can save taxes in the years leading to retirement?

9. Do you understand how a Family Farm Partnership could create tax savings?

10. If you farm through a corporation here are some considerations:

    10.1 Does your corporate structure ensure that your shares can "roll" to children in the event of your death rather than being taxed?

    10.2 Do you know if your shares will qualify for the lifetime Capital Gains Exemption?

10.3 Have you obtained advice about whether you need a separate holding corporation?

10.4 Will your corporate structure allow for the most tax-effective transfer of the operation to family members?

10.5 Do you understand how corporately held insurance can create a tax efficient succession plan?

As you can see, these are just a few of the questions that need to be addressed.

A discussion with a skilled Family Wealth Advisor will bring many more questions to the forefront.

WARNING: What if you are separated, divorced or thinking about either?

The following is just an introduction and should not be construed as tax advice.

As a family wealth advisor, I have seen how marriage breakdown and separation/divorce can wreak havoc on relationships and with it impact the long-term health of farm and farm relationships.

Married life is supposed to be forever, but according to Canada government statistics, some 40% of marriages dissolve before they reach their 30th anniversary.[3]

[3] https://www.bdo.ca/en-ca/insights/tax/tax-articles/tax-implications-of-separation-or-divorce-for-a-business-owner-manager/

Separation or divorce can have a significant impact on the health, stability and future of your farm.

How you approach separation and the division of personal and farm assets will have long-term tax implications for you, your spouse and your farm.

Canadian tax rules for spouses are very clear and specific and differ from civil definitions.

Three tax areas which will impact your farm are:

1. Spousal attribution rules,

2. Spousal transfer Rollover and

3. Capital gains Exemptions.

If you are separated, divorced or considering either, please contact your Wealth Advisor who will put you in touch with a competent tax professional.

As you can see this analysis process will require a lot of thought and planning.

You will find a sample **Farm Wealth Planning Checklist** – Chapter 21

CHAPTER 6

STEP 3:
COMMIT TO CREATING
A FARM TRANSITION PLAN

3. Commit to creating a plan

After examining some of the questions in previous chapters, you can see how important it is to make a plan.

Your next step should be to commit to creating a plan.

This means setting time aside to compile a list of all the questions (and answers if you have them) about every aspect of your farm business and personal life.

It's not about having time, but about making time.

In the same way, you don't always have time to play with your grandchildren, you know you will make time to create memories and form bonds that will be remembered for many years to come.

Yes, the process may seem overwhelming.

However, just like every task you've ever taken on, it begins with that first step, that first shovelful, that first foundation.

How do you eat an elephant? One mouthful at a time. It may seem that this thinking and planning process is just like eating an elephant.

As you examine all the different parts of your farm business, you will soon realize that your lifetime of effort has created a living, breathing entity that will provide for you and your family for many years to come.

That accomplishment is something to be celebrated.

All those early, lonely hours, all that blood and sweat and all those tears have resulted in tangible and intangible assets of which you can be proud.

You have one more step, one more challenge ahead of you. To structure your business in such a way as to maximize the benefit for you and your family.

CHAPTER 7

STEP 4:
CREATE A SOLID WEALTH FOUNDATION

4. Create a solid wealth foundation

This is all about you and your family's needs.

Your plan should also help determine what you *need* to reach your objective.

For example:

1. Do you need to enhance the value of your farm before you can sell it?

2. Does the future of your farm include your children or extended family?

3. Do you need to minimize future taxes so that the sale or transition of your farm will not complicate things?

4. Do you need a higher return on your investments or less risk so that your wealth will be more secure?

5. Do you need a will and estate plan to ensure your family will be taken care of should anything unexpected happen?

6. Do you need to simplify your farm operations because you are spread too thin? Or do you need to expand and diversify to prevent all your eggs from staying in one basket?

These are just a few of the questions to ponder.

Like many farmers, your wealth is tied up in your farm. Once you have sold your farm, you need to create a solid investment foundation to manage the proceeds from the sale of your farm.

You will want to examine your needs with respect to investing the proceeds from the sale of your farm or the cash you put aside before transferring your farm to your children to secure your retirement.

This will involve examining and quantifying your:

- risk tolerance
- liquidity requirements
- growth expectations
- insurance and annuity requirements
- income tax characteristics
- anticipated changes in lifestyle
- economic variables such as inflation and market volatility.

Because you have been busy running your farm, you will probably not have spent much time examining long-term investment and wealth strategies.

What information you will have gleaned along the way will probably have come from accountants, lawyers and all those talking heads on TV who inhabit the financial channels and disseminate all that advice - some of which can be contradictory.

Where does one go for good, reliable advice?

Because we can't be experts in every field, we will need to speak with qualified, knowledgeable advisors.

Let me direct you to **Chapter 13 The Role of Advisors** where I will discuss in detail how to select a qualified and knowledgeable advisor.

CHAPTER 8

STEP 5:
DESIGN YOUR FARM
TRANSITION PLAN

5. Design your farm transition plan

In the same way an architect helps you design and build a home or farm building, you need to have a plan designed by wealth planning professionals.

This plan will protect and enhance the value of your farm and minimize taxes in preparation for sale or transfer of your farm.

Up until now, you will have been using your team of accountants and lawyers to structure and protect your farm.

A farm transition, however, can be a much more complex subject as you are learning from the previous chapters.

This requires a level of specialization that most lawyers and accountants don't have.

This is where a Wealth Advisor comes in.

A qualified, experienced and knowledgeable Wealth Advisor does not operate in a vacuum.

Over the years, the advisor will have built a team of wealth planning professionals on whom they can draw to help you design your plan.

The larger your farm business, the more complex the team will be.

They will work together with your lawyer and accountant(s) to analyze all possible solutions and design the best plan to preserve and enhance your wealth, and conceive a simple path for you to follow to achieve your desired future.

CHAPTER 9

STEP 6:
EXECUTE YOUR PLAN

6. Execute your plan

Once you've developed *The Plan*, it will be time to implement *The Plan*.

This will involve meetings – lots of meetings between you and your advisors.

Meetings to discuss *The Plan* and then meetings to begin implementing *The Plan*.

Meetings to document any major changes in your personal or financial situation that require an adjustment to *The Plan*.

This may take months, and maybe even years if you start soon enough or have a number of years to go before you want to go out to pasture.

You must be aware that *The Plan* is not fixed in stone but is a living and flexible document that may require changes and improvements.

Every year, all levels of governments play around with the rules and regulations that affect our lives.

With every federal budget, tax relief is provided or tax regulations are increased.

Keeping up with all those changes requires knowledge (your advisors) and decisions on your part to modify your plan to maximize the benefit to you and your family.

The most important characteristic you will need is **patience**.

Patience with the process and patience with all the people in the process who will need to be involved and kept up to date.

During this time, hidden family stresses and issues may arise. Some family members may change their minds about the details while others may no longer want to be involved.

Also, see my comments about separation or divorce in Chapter 5.

CHAPTER 10

STEP 7:
ACHIEVE YOUR DESIRED
FUTURE

7. Achieve your desired future

Whew!

The implementation process is sometimes lengthy as the material is intense. It takes time to decide on the most efficient course of action for you to follow.

Once *The Plan* is complete, it will now be up to you to follow the steps in *Your Plan*.

Remember all those dreams we discussed in Chapter 4? By now you should see them coming to fruition.

Your long-suffering spouse is encouraging you to take a month or two and travel.

Isn't it time to let go and let the farm get along without you?

It's very hard, but you deserve the time off. Who knows you may even like it.

And the grandkids? They want to see you more often.

Admit it. You want to see them as well - for a while.

CHAPTER 11

STEP 8:
SHARE YOUR FAMILY'S WEALTH

8. Share your family's wealth

You've built your nest egg.

You've prepared for yourself and your family for the next generation(s).

You also want to help others.

With wise administration and strategic tax planning, you will be able to support your favourite charitable institution.

Whether it's the local food bank, a religious institution or funding high school and college scholarships and bursaries, your support will reap dividends for years to come.

Typically, giving can be achieved in four ways.

1. Giving your money directly.

You have found a cause, an organization or person who could use your financial assistance. You take out your check book or some cash and give it to them directly. Alternatively, you can give them securities that you own.

You may be offered a tax-deductible receipt if you give to an organization. If you give cash directly to a disadvantaged individual, you will not receive a tax deduction but you will receive their thanks and you will feel warm fuzzies because you have made a difference in someone's life.

In some cases, your giving will be anonymous, but in other times you will use your giving as a model and example for your family. Having compassion and being charitable is a valuable character trait.

*"We make a living by what we get, but
we make a life by what we give."*
Winston Churchill

2. You can give by volunteering your time.

Volunteering for a charity or a non-profit models responsible stewardship of time. Giving your time and energy to serve in a soup kitchen, for example, benefits the community. It also allows you to make a personal connection with the organization's workers and benefactors. In some cases, you receive immediate positive feedback from your involvement.

> *"Volunteering is at the very core of being a human. No one has made it through life without someone else's help."*
>
> *Heather French Henry*

3. Purchasing a life insurance policy

When you purchase a life insurance policy and name a charity as the sole beneficiary you generate a disproportionate benefit for that organization. The amount they receive will in all likelihood be much larger than you will ever be able to give them in cash or securities.

> *"The best way to find yourself is to lose yourself in the service of others."*
>
> *Mahatma Gandhi*

4. Establishing a charitable trust

Besides the immediate tax deductions, capital gains reductions and reduction of estate and income taxes upon your death, a charitable trust provides a longer benefit to the charity of your choice. A lump sum invested on behalf of a charity will pay longer dividends than just a single lump sum.

"We rise by lifting others."
Robert Ingersoll

CHAPTER 12

HOW DO I DO ALL THIS?

About Adrian Spitters
FCSI, CFP, FMA
Senior Wealth Advisor

Farm Life has always been an important part of my world. I grew up on a dairy farm on Nicomen Island near Mission, BC and have immediate family and relatives operating dairy, poultry and crop farms.

As co-executor (with two brothers) of my father's estate, I know all too well the result of not having a proper farm transition plan in place.

Our dad had a poorly executed, unworkable Will and a non-existent farm succession plan.

This led to family discord. Despite receiving the majority of the assets, the brother who inherited the farm suffered financial distress and became insolvent.

A proper transition plan would have helped him get the financial and farm management training he needed.

Today, I work as a Senior Wealth Advisor with Assante Capital Management Ltd., a leading Canadian wealth management firm with extensive experience in family business transitions. In my work with the **Assante Ag Group**, I provide wealth advisory services to farm and business families. This includes helping them grow, protect and preserve their family assets, wealth and legacy.

In my 30 years in the business, I've seen: that all Canadians, especially farmers, need and want personalized financial advice that helps them achieve their life goals.

It is very clear to me that whether you have a transition plan in place or not, one day you will transfer your farm to your children, extended family or sell to a third party. The question is, will it be on your terms **(voluntarily)**, or someone else's **(involuntarily)**?

To that end, I have acquired great expertise by working with the wealth planning specialists I encounter as a member of the **Assante Ag Group**.

I specialize in developing specific and personalized strategies for each of my farm clients.

I work to enhance their knowledge, provide guidance, and create peace of mind for each of them to enjoy.

CHAPTER 13

THE ROLE OF ADVISORS

Getting the Help You Need: Building Your Transition Team

Throughout this book, I've written about talking with advisors and experts.

Successfully planning for and ultimately selling your farm will almost certainly require some expert help. There are so many legal, accounting, tax, and insurance implications that it's all but impossible for you to do it all on your own.

Getting a qualified valuation of your farm is also vital. *Fair market value* (for example) can be a very sticky issue with tax authorities, and trying to hand over your farm to your immediate or extended family at a "good" price can have unintended (and serious) consequences.

Most farmers feel busy enough without having to contemplate the complex – and sometimes unpleasant – possibility of selling or transitioning their farm someday. But unless they're planning on living (or working!) forever, "then an ounce of prevention is worth a pound of cure." You are best served by engaging wealth management professionals to help make the process simple, easy, and *effective*.

Of course, you *could* work with individual professionals in all these areas (legal, accounting, tax, etc.) You may even believe you already have a plan for each of these areas.

Warning

But there's a potential pitfall to that approach of which you must be aware. When working with many disparate individuals, you could end up subject to conflicting and sometimes incomplete advice.

The Result?

You end up making essentially "random" investment, insurance, tax, trust, farm succession planning, and estate planning decisions that are all in isolation of each other. This will lead to a collection of investments, insurance, business, and trust structures that are fragmented, confusing, and not particularly tax efficient. When this happens, you become vulnerable to missed opportunities, unnecessary expenses, and unforeseen tax liabilities. It's not an exaggeration to say that the consequences could be catastrophic.

That's why an *integrated* transition plan is necessary. It's the only way to ensure everything is done right and nothing is missed.

There's another reason to hire a professional transition team to assist you. You see, some farmers never *really* retire, especially if they have transitioned the farm to their children. They still keep an eye on how the farm is run because they want to make sure their retirement remains secure. This creates a lot of stress both on the farmer and on his/her children. The farmer can't let things go, and the children can't make decisions for themselves.

Here's the good news. With an experienced transition team, you don't have to keep a never-ending eye on your farm, because you don't have to worry about keeping your retirement secure. By working with a team to create a transition plan, you'll be able to extract enough assets from your farm to set up a separate retirement portfolio *before* you ever quit working. And you'll have increased confidence that your retirement is secure.

Let me direct you to **Chapter 27, Your Optimal Portfolio Solution™** where I will discuss in detail how your retirement portfolio should be built, so you can retire with peace of mind.

How Can You Find That Experienced Advisor?

Let's first talk about wealth and wealth management.

What Is Wealth Management and <u>Why Should You Care?</u>

Wealth management is more than just investment advice.

Wealth management encompasses all parts of a person's personal and business life. A person's wealth is not just what they have in their investment portfolio – it's everything they have accumulated: their home, their cottage, their business, other business interests, investment property, etc.

To manage all these assets requires the advice of multiple

professionals from accountants, lawyers, investment advisors, realtors, bankers, mortgage brokers, insurance agents, financial planners, estate planners and many more.

Most of these advisors usually work in isolation of each other. This isolation can result in conflicting and sometimes incomplete advice, leading to bad financial decisions that happen in isolation of a person's overall financial objectives and needs.

The reality is, while most people have an investment plan, an insurance plan, a tax plan, and maybe even a farm succession plan and/or estate plan, these plans were most likely done for them at different times by different advisors in isolation of each other.

The result is a collection of investments, insurance, business and trust structures that are fragmented and not tax-efficient, resulting in missed opportunities, and unnecessary expense, unforeseen tax liability, duplication of obligations and at worst, catastrophic consequences.

Rather than trying to make sense of the sometimes-conflicting advice from these professionals, farm families can benefit from a holistic approach to managing their wealth with a single advisor who coordinates all the services they need to manage their wealth and plan for their own and/or their family's current and future needs.

Wealth Advisors start by developing a plan that will grow

and protect their clients' wealth based on their clients' personal financial situation, goals, comfort level, risk tolerance and needs.

This would encompass an investment plan to manage their investments, a risk plan to manage the risks to their wealth and livelihood, a personal tax plan to manage the tax implications of managing their personal wealth, a farm tax and succession plan to plan the sale or transition of their farm to new owners when they retire in a tax-efficient manner, and an estate plan to transfer their assets to the next generation tax-efficiently that also meets their wishes on who gets what and how.

Once all these plans are created, the Wealth Advisor works with their clients' own network of professionals to implement the various components of their plan and then meets with them on a regular basis to review and monitor the progress of their plans.

These plans are revised and updated when needed. Wealth Advisors touch every aspect of their clients' wealth from growing, protecting, and transferring their wealth to the next generation.

Most financial advisors are not Wealth Advisors. They do not have the knowledge or access to integrated wealth management services.

So how do you find a Wealth Advisor that can offer all the services mentioned above?

Good question!

Let's talk about the **7 Key Questions Every Financial Advisor MUST Be Able to Answer** before you hire them to manage your wealth so that you can achieve financial freedom, security and peace of mind!

Now… you may be expecting a series of questions like:

"Do you have any samples of the types of portfolios you recommend?"

"What are your fees?"

"Can you show me testimonials?"

"How are your fees charged?"

"What is your track record?"

And all those are good questions. Any financial advisor worth their salt will have ready responses in place.

As someone who has been there in the trenches with the best of them, let me lay on you some queries the average financial advisor ISN'T expecting… which will enable you to see who's ready to advise you on your money and family wealth.

Ok here we go…

I have prepared a list of questions that you can ask. To access these questions, go to **www.7keyquestions.ca**

DOWNLOAD MY FREE BOOK

Do you have the right financial advisor working for you? Not sure?

Find out in my new book:

Who's Investing Your Money?–

Learn How to Ask the Right Questions to Select the Best Financial Advisor for Your Situation

To get your free book visit:
www.whosinvestingyourmoney.com

In this next section I will be discussing some specific issues in some detail to demonstrate the wealth and breadth of knowledge required to effectively structure the farm transition.

Feel free to contact me for specifics.

(604) 855-6846

CHAPTER 14

SELLING YOUR FARM

Essentially, you have two basic options for exiting your farming business.

1. The **first** is to sell to another person or another farmer. It's an arms-length transaction, and as such will often require the most effort and discipline. But it's also the option that usually provides the highest financial reward. These days, however, many farmers don't end up choosing to sell their farms. Instead, they take the second option.

2. The **second** – and more common – option is to transfer or sell your farm to the next generation of your family.

Management expert Peter Drucker, perhaps a little tongue in cheek, calls this **"the final test of greatness"** for business leaders... and that includes farmers.

Family dynamics make this choice arguably the most complex, and studies show this transfer to be successful in only around 30% of cases.[4]

Just 10% of businesses successfully reach the 3rd generation![5] However, the right amount of openness, clarity and respect between family members, along with legally sound transfer/sale documents, will go a long way towards making this option a great triumph.

[4] Family Business Institute http://www.familybusinessinstitute.com/index.php/succession-planning/

[5] Family Business Institute http://www.familybusinessinstitute.com/index.php/succession-planning/

CHAPTER 15

TAX STRATEGIES FOR FARMERS

In this chapter, I will make some broad observations.

As with the other subjects discussed, your mileage may vary.

This too will be an introduction and should not be construed as giving tax advice. That is best left to tax lawyers and business tax specialists.

Tax strategies deserve special consideration for two very broad reasons.

The **first** is the tax-saving advantages that can be gained by planning properly long before you sell your farm.

The **second** reason is the not-so-pleasant tax repercussions that will occur should you sell or transition your farm improperly, particularly under the watchful eyes of the CRA (Canada Revenue Agency).

Fortunately, farmers have several options when it comes to minimizing the tax consequences of selling or transitioning their farm.

Have a look at the **Appendix** for a detailed look at two important strategies that require advance planning to be effective.

- **Estate Freeze** – Appendix A

- **Family Trusts** - Appendix B

Here are two important ones to know:

Option 1) Tax-free Rollover

Remember how you can either sell or transition your farm? Imagine you decided to take the 2nd option, which is to transfer your farm to someone in your family.

The Income Tax Act of Canada allows for qualified farms to be transferred to children on a tax-free basis. In other words, you would not have to pay a tax on the transfer itself. Certain conditions have to be met for your farm to qualify, but this is certainly an option worth looking into.

Tax-free rollovers are very common among farmers. That's because farmers have special tax rules to adhere to which are different than the rules for general business owners. As a result, these types of rollovers apply only to farmers and fishermen.

Option 2) Capital Gains Exemption

This is perhaps the most popular tax planning technique.

With a Capital Gains Exemption or CGE, you can sell qualified shares of a farm corporation and earn an exemption from having to pay a capital gains tax on the gains of up to $1,000,000 per spouse or individual family member with an ownership position in the farm and farm assets.

Note that for your children to qualify, advanced planning is required.

The $1,000,000 Capital Gains Exemption is also available to farm individuals on the sale of qualified farm property.

Qualified farm property includes:
- Farm land and buildings
- Shares in a family farm corporation
- An interest in a family farm partnership
- Quota

As with the tax-free rollover mentioned above, certain conditions apply. For example, if your farm corporation has excess cash or assets that are not actively being used in the daily operation of the farm, this may disqualify you from being eligible.

Also, if some of your farm assets do not qualify, steps will need to be taken to ensure that the farm qualifies. This can take years to do, meaning you should plan now to ensure all of your assets qualify.

Every farm and farmer is unique, and so is each farmer's tax situation. Remember, farmers have special tax rules that differ from those of non-farm businesses.

Also, see my comments about tax implications of separation or divorce in Chapter 5.

A Wealth Advisor will have an army of experts available to help you navigate the dangerous waters of the Tax Code.

Here is an example of how wealth advisors are valuable allies in the fight to reduce taxes.

A retired farm couple owned a holding company that held the proceeds from the sale of their farm quota. By claiming their personal lifetime capital gains exemptions, they were able to extract capital out of their holding company.

However, they still had approximately $550,000 remaining in their holding company.

Their children had no interest in taking over the farm so the money could not be rolled over to their children. The couple had significant assets outside of their holding company, so there was no need to withdraw money from the holding company to maintain their lifestyle.

My clients wanted to wind down the holding company as it was a dead asset as far as they were concerned and a potentially significant tax liability to their children.

With a life expectancy of over 15 years, the couple saw that their assets would easily grow to over $1,000,000.

Years ago, the farm couple had purchased a $500,000 joint last-to-die insurance policy as an estate planning tool to reduce personal taxes on their death. I had an insurance expert review their policies. Upon reviewing their current tax situation and seeing the couple wanted to reduce the estate tax liability of their holding company, the advisor recommended a tax-free asset transfer.

The couple would sell their personal policy to their corporation. We had an actuary review their policy to determine the current market value of the policy. Based on their age and health, it was determined that the policy was worth approximately $250,000. This meant that they would receive approximately $250,000 from their corporation by selling the policy to the company. When they pass away, the proceeds from the insurance policy would be received by the corporation and passed through the Capital Dividend account tax-free to their beneficiaries.

The couple incurred some personal taxes on the gain in value between the time they purchased the insurance policy to when they sold it to their company, but the tax liability was minimal, and the tax-free benefit was substantial.

CHAPTER 16

ENOUGH FOR YOU AND YOUR FAMILY'S FUTURE

An important part of the transition process is to create a comprehensive plan encompassing all aspects of your financial life. By understanding what specifically about money is important to you, and how much you will need to achieve your goals, dreams, and lifestyle needs, you will have a better idea of when work can become optional for you instead of mandatory. This also helps give you the peace of mind you need in order to ensure you are exercising sound judgment when the time comes to sell or transition your farm.

Whenever you *do* decide to retire, it's critical that you have sufficient assets to provide a secure future for yourself and your family. There are a lot of factors to consider when it comes to this step, but there are two, in particular, that should be near the top of every list:

Income and Expenses

Why are these two so important?

To put it bluntly, it all comes down to this simple rule. *You cannot retire successfully unless your income is **more** than your outgo.*

It sounds like a no-brainer, and it is. Yet I can't count the number of people I meet every week who have no idea what their income will be after their retirement... never mind if it will be more than their expenses. These people want to retire; they hope to retire, but they don't know if they really can.

Of course, there's more to retiring successfully than just being able to pay the bills.

Retirement is all about finally having the time and opportunity to try new things, go new places, and learn new skills. Here again is why income is so important. All those things cost money. So how do you know what you can do after retirement if you don't know whether you'll have the money to do it?

This is what you need to do. First, sit down and calculate what your income and expenses are *now*. Here are some questions you need to answer.

What is your monthly income after taxes?

If you live off the farm:

- How much do you pay in monthly utilities?
- How much debt do you have, and what are your monthly payments like? Remember, this can include mortgage payments, car payments, credit card payments, etc.
- How much do you spend on automobile insurance, home insurance, gas, and other regular expenses? Don't forget to consider any out-of-pocket medical costs.

Step 1:

Once you've tallied those numbers, subtract your expenses from your income. Whatever number remains is what's immediately available to set aside for retirement.

Now determine what expenses might change after retirement. For example:

What expenses will you have more difficulty paying once you are no longer drawing regular income from your farm?

What expenses do you currently take for granted that are covered by your farm that will no longer be covered once you live off the farm? This would include such expenses as property taxes, hydro, phone, property maintenance, vehicle gas, and maintenance, etc.

What expenses do you currently have that will *decrease* after retirement?

What is your current tax bracket? Will it change after you retire and start earning less income?

Now comes the home stretch.

Finish these final steps:

Step 2:

Take your existing expenses then add the expenses that will go *up* after retirement. Next, subtract the expenses that will go *down*. Hold on to that number for a moment.

Step 3:

Calculate the amount of income you expect to receive from Canada Pension Plan (CPP), Old Age Security (OAS) and any retirement accounts you have, like a Registered Retirement Savings Plan (RRSP), investment accounts, or Tax-Free Savings Account (TFSA). Then subtract the tax you'll owe on these accounts once you start using them.

But remember; the order in which you draw income from these accounts is very important, because it will have a significant impact on how much net income you will receive in retirement and how long your retirement income will last.

You also need to consider the effect of inflation on your income and expenses. You may think you have enough when you retire. However, you must factor in the official average annual rate of inflation, which is 2%.

In addition, retirees often find that their personal rate of inflation is much higher. Also, be sure to factor in a realistic rate of return on your retirement investments, or you may find after 20 years of retirement that you do not have enough to achieve all your retirement goals. The good news is that we can show you how long your money will last with inflation calculated into your plan.

Take the final number from Step 3 and combine it with the amount you can save from Step 1. Then compare it to the number from Step 2. Steps 1 and 3 combined is your income after retirement. Step 2 is your expenses.

Which number is higher?

Keep in mind that every number you reach from this exercise is just a loose estimate. Too loose, in fact, to make financial decisions by, but at the very least, this should get you thinking. And if you'd like a much more concrete projection of your income and expenses after retirement, all you have to do is give me a call.

Helping people plan for retirement is my specialty. I'd be happy to sit down with you, ask some questions, and prepare a comprehensive estimate.

Just contact me at **(604) 855-6846** and we can schedule a time to meet.

In the meantime, just remember this fundamental truth: ***you cannot retire successfully unless your income is more than your expenses.*** Remember, too, that your income should be enough to cover your wants as well as your needs. So, start thinking about it today. It's a complex topic, but you've got plenty of time if you start working on it now.

To sum up, creating a formal farm transition plan should provide you with a blueprint of *what* your goals in life will cost, *how* to be able to afford them, and *when* to execute various strategies designed to help you achieve them.

CHAPTER 17

PREPARING YOUR FAMILY

Preparing your family
for a smooth and efficient transition

Have you ever heard of the "**Six W**" questions? They go like this: **Who, What, When, Where, Why,** and **How.** If you are planning on transitioning your farm to a member (or members) of your family, each of these questions will need to be answered...and it's important that your family be involved. Too often, farmers make all the decisions by themselves, springing them on family members at the last minute.

This can lead to mistakes, stress, and resentment…and ultimately, to a failing farm.

Answering the "**Six W**" questions isn't easy, but fortunately, you don't have to do it alone. While I focus mainly on the *financial* aspects of transitioning your farm, there are professionals out there who specialize in the family and emotional aspects.

Please contact me if you have questions about the family and emotional aspects of farm transition.

CHAPTER 18

HOW CAN I HELP YOU?

Our Family Farm Transition Process

Helping farmers create the kind of farm transition plan described above is my goal. I do this through the 8-step process outlined earlier.

Farmers who dream of retiring someday, are encouraged to sit down with me to discuss their farm transition plan.

Here's How It Works

The moment you walk through my door you'll be treated like a client. I'll have a cup of coffee, or tea, waiting if you want it. When we sit down together, my philosophy is first to *listen* rather than speak.

I want to know about your goals, your dreams, your needs. What do you want to do with your farm? What do you want to protect? It's my job to learn these details. Only then will I suggest a possible course of action.

In this way, we can help you **visualize** your desired future. Then, we'll take stock of what you have to work with and what obstacles need to be overcome to reach that future.

We'll examine and list all your **Strengths, Weaknesses, Opportunities**, and **Threats (SWOT)**. This is how we **analyze your current reality**.

From here, farmers can decide whether they truly want to **commit to creating a plan**. Because they now have a greater understanding of what they want *and* what they have to overcome, we find at this point that most farmers are more excited and motivated to create a plan than ever before.

For any transition to be effective, farmers first need to ensure they have a **solid wealth foundation** on which to retire.

This is why we recommend that farmers take advantage of our **Integrated Wealth Management** services through Assante Private Client, a division of CI Private Counsel LP.

Integrated Wealth Management

"Integrated Wealth Management" means combining *every* aspect of your financial life into an overall plan.

This involves four main aspects:

- Your investment selections
- Your asset allocation
- Your taxes
- Your estate

Some farmers may have a few investments here and there, or have had their taxes looked at by a professional, or filled out a will several years ago. But most farmers don't have a plan in place for *all* these things.

Farmers who enlist my services, enjoy having each of these aspects working *in concert* together rather than separately. For example, doesn't it make more sense to know how your investments will affect your taxes, and vice versa? Doesn't it make more sense to factor in how your *heirs'* taxes will be impacted when your estate is passed onto them?

The fact of the matter is that most of your wealth is tied up in your farm. Selling or transitioning your farm will have a major impact on your overall wealth.

That's why it's so important to integrate every aspect of your wealth into your plan. It's the only way to ensure said impact will be positive instead of negative. Furthermore, once you have sold or transitioned your farm, you will need to have an investment strategy in place to better manage the proceeds from the sale, or the lump sum you extracted from the farm to secure your retirement.

Many farmers like to keep a constant eye on the farm even after they have technically handed off the day-to-day management duties. This is because they want to make sure their retirement remains secure.

By having an Integrated Wealth Management Plan in place, you'll be able to spend more time *enjoying* retirement and less time worrying about it. That's because your plan will likely recommend setting aside sufficient assets into a separate retirement account *outside* of your farm before retirement.

This is your retirement nest egg. More importantly, your plan will specify how much "sufficient" actually is. This way, once your account is large enough, you'll be able to generate income *before* you retire from your farm.

You know what that means: greater peace of mind. With your own retirement secure, you can more readily forego the daily grind and let your heirs run the farm and make decisions for themselves.

Ultimately, having an Integrated Wealth Management Plan means enjoying the fruits of your hard-earned labor, while your children begin making decisions on their own.

To put it simply, participating in our Integrated Wealth Management program will enable you to have a **solid wealth foundation** on which to retire.

Your Farm Transition Plan

Once your wealth foundation is in place, we can then **design a specific, personal transition plan for you**. During this process, we will connect with any other professionals you are already working with – attorneys, accountants, etc. – to create the simplest, most direct path from where you are to where you want to be.

Remember, your plan should help you:

1. Determine the value of your farm
2. Find the right buyer
3. Choose the right time to sell
4. Decide whether to transition your farm to a family member or sell to a non-related party

5. Determine whether selling your farm will bring in enough proceeds to fund your retirement and other financial goals.
6. Ensure the orderly payment and transition of ownership/management of your farm to your successor/heir.
7. Minimize the taxes that come from selling your farm
8. Ensure you have sufficient assets to secure you and your family's future.

Once your plan is created, it will be time to **execute your plan**. But the responsibility shouldn't fall on your shoulders alone – we'll be there to hold your hand through the entire process. We do that by meeting regularly with you to review your plan and assess your progress. We will also work closely with your legal and accounting teams to implement all the financial, legal, insurance, and tax strategies your plan contains.

Then comes the best part. Executing your plan will enable you to reach your destination. To **achieve your desired future**. Even then, however, our work is not done. We'll meet with you every three-to-six months, or more often if necessary, to check in on how you're doing. We'll also document any major changes in your financial situation that require us to adjust your plan.

Finally, we will assist you with the eighth and final step of the Farm Transition Process, which is to **share your family's wealth**. By this point, you have built a solid wealth foundation, sold or transferred your farm, and achieved your desired future. In this final step, we continue to meet with you *and* your heirs on an as-needed basis to ensure that your family's future – and your legacy – endures for generations to come.

Our Clients

If you are interested in learning more about our Farm Transition Process and Integrated Wealth Management Services, I'd love to hear from you!

In our experience, the services we offer work best with certain types of farm families. That's why our clients are part of a select group of farm families with a certain net worth who have decided to invest a portion of their assets with Assante Private Client. Assante Private Client is a division of CI Private Counsel LP, which houses the Wealth Planning Group (a specialized team to whom many clients of Assante Ag Group advisors have access).

Of course, whether you choose to become a client or not, it's always a good idea to at least come in for a free consultation. Together, we can help you understand some of your options and which path is best for you. From there, you can decide whether or not to continue with our planning process by becoming an investment client.

Learn more about how Assante can help you grow, preserve, and protect your retirement assets, please call me at (604) 855-6846 or email me at **aspitters@assante.com.**

Summary

It should be clear by now that to reach your retirement goals; it may become necessary to sell your farm someday.

To sell your farm in a timely, cost-effective, and *profitable* manner, you need to have a farm transition plan.

It's this plan that will give you the step by step instructions needed to ensure the orderly transition of your farm to your buyer and/or your heirs, minimize taxes, and ensure you have sufficient assets for both you and your family's future.

CHAPTER 19

HOW DO YOU START THE PROCESS?

Do Not Do It Alone!

The world of finance has gotten more complex than ever. It takes years of time and training to master all the intricacies of financial planning, to say nothing of the laws and regulations that seem to change every year.

As a farmer, your time and energy should be spent on one thing: your farm.

That's why it's so crucial to choose an experienced, qualified wealth management expert to help you.

Such an expert can answer your questions and look closely at your farm before suggesting the best course of action. An expert can do the legwork and manage your plan, giving you confidence and peace of mind.

To demonstrate what a farm transition plan would look like, and how it would fit within our overall **Integrated Wealth Management services**, I'm currently offering a free consultation to farmers in Fraser Valley.

If you are reading this book in another province and want to meet with an Assante Ag Group Advisor, I can arrange an introduction for you.

All we'll do is sit down, have a cup of coffee, and look at your goals and needs. I'll explain some of the things you'll need to consider and where to get started. There's no obligation on your part. If you need further assistance from me, I'd be thrilled to provide it. If not, no matter. I'm just happy to help in any way I can!

If you want to take me up on my offer, just give me a call at (604) 855-6846, or e-mail me at **aspitters@assante.com.** We'll set up a time to meet whenever is most convenient for you. Keep in mind that the sooner we meet, the sooner you can have a plan in place.

And remember…

If your goal is to quit working someday, creating a plan is a must.

Thinking about your future is a must.

Taking action is a must, too.

Don't waste another day. Start now!

Call me today: (604) 855-6846

CHAPTER 20

ADRIAN SPITTERS AND THE ASSANTE AG GROUP

Assante Ag Group

Your Farm. Your Family. Your Future.

The Assante Ag Group is a national farm advisory group that assists Canadian farm families in the areas of *tax planning, retirement planning, and wealth transfer*. As a member of the Assante Ag Group, I am part of a team of highly experienced and trusted wealth planning specialists that include lawyers and accountants with knowledge and experience in the tax and estate planning issues that affect farmers.

Taxation represents the single largest expense and loss of capital in the lives of many farm families, particularly in the retirement phase. As a member of the Assante Ag Group, I work directly with the farm family to help them understand the complex tax and financial issues that need to be addressed to minimize loss of farm wealth when important transitions or transactions occur.

Tax, Financial and Estate Planning

As an Assante Ag Group advisor, my main focus and strengths are tax minimization, wealth planning and estate planning, including:

- Planning for the tax efficient transfer of the family farm to the next generation;
- Pre-retirement planning for the tax-efficient sale of the farm equipment, inventory and other assets;
- Planning tax efficient business structures for the family farm and other ventures;
- Personal tax and estate planning;
- Financial and retirement planning.

My approach is to bring together not only tax, estate and financial planning, but also tax efficient managed wealth solutions and insurance strategies, all personalized to meet the unique needs and values of each client family.

Coordinating Professional Advice

The busy lives of farm families can seem further complicated by the necessary involvement of professionals from various disciplines, such as accountants and lawyers. As a member of the Assante Ag Group, I provide a comprehensive plan that coordinates the services of these professionals. This plan helps coordinate the implementation with the client family's accountant and lawyer, and continues to monitor the client family's tax and financial affairs thereafter and through the retirement years.

Financial Matters for Farmers – An invitation from Adrian Spitters

Initial Introduction

As an Assante Ag Group Wealth Advisor, I provide a free initial consultation to introduce our wealth management program and to review your investment portfolio and financial situation for opportunities and income tax strategies.

What You Can Expect

- Comprehensive financial planning encompassing tax, insurance, estate, and succession planning based on your long-term goals while still providing for the short-term needs of you and your family
- A personal investment plan based on your goals, tax situation, income requirements, and risk tolerance
- Access to tax lawyers, accountants, and insurance, estate and investment specialists
- Identification, explanation and coordination of tax and estate planning strategies to be implemented by your professional advisors
- Ongoing monitoring of your investments and regular reviews of your financial, tax, and estate plans

A Commitment to Farm Families

I am committed to maintaining the high levels of proficiency and expertise required to provide professional advice.

Adrian Spitters •

Senior Wealth Advisor •

Assante Capital Management Ltd.

604 - 855 - 6846 •

aspitters@assante.com

Web: www.yourfarmtransitionadvisor.ca

CHAPTER 21

FARM
WEALTH PLANNING CHECKLIST

Here is a sample
Farm Wealth Planning Check List

Wealth planning is more than investment returns

It is a process to maximize what you have, provide for your future and effectively pass it on.

Wealth planning is not just for the "wealthy"

It is something that everyone should do. It is never too early or too late to plan.

Wealth planning provides a financial framework for your life and beyond.

It is personal. It is customised. And it works.

BIG PICTURE

My 3 biggest concerns today are:

1. _____

_____

_____

2. _____

_____

_____

3. _____

_____

_____

What are your most important planning objectives	NOT Important	Important	VERY Important
Identifying all the issues you need to consider: financial, retirement, tax, succession or sale issues			
Having enough money to sustain your desired lifestyle in retirement			
Structuring your affairs to minimize tax now, at retirement and on death			
Maximizing returns in your investment portfolio			
Deciding whether/when you will be ready for a change in lifestyle			
Passing the farm to your farming child(ren) while balancing non-farm child(ren)'s interests			
Taking care of others in the event of your illness, disability or death - parents, children, grandchildren			
Leaving a personal legacy - values, traditions, ethics, life lessons and inheritance			
Paying for children's or grandchildren's education			
Maximizing a gift/bequest to your favorite charity			
Avoiding probate fees			
Avoiding family conflict after you're gone			

Retirement Planning	NOT Important	Important	VERY Important
Do you know when you can financially afford to retire?			
Do you have a plan for when, or if, you will retire from active farming & a clear vision of your life in retirement?			
Do you and your spouse agree on what your lifestyle will be in retirement?			
Do you know how much you need to receive on an after-tax basis from the sale of your farm to enable you to maintain your current lifestyle in retirement?			
Do you know how much you can spend monthly/annually during retirement without outliving savings?			
Do you sometimes wonder if it is important to diversify some wealth into some non-farm assets?			
Do you wonder if completely eliminating all income tax every year might not be the best retirement planning?			
Do you think you can minimize current taxes and also save for retirement at the same time?			
Do you know how to hold retirement savings so they don't interfere with farm tax planning opportunities?			
Do you know how many years in advance a farmer must start planning for retirement?			

Retirement Planning	NOT Important	Important	VERY Important
Do you know why is it harder for a farmer to defer income in the years leading up to retirement?			

Will you need to rely on government pension for income?
  * should you apply for CPP early?
 	
  * will your OAS benefits be subject to the claw back?			

Do you know which retirement income sources to spend first and how to minimize taxes?			
Do you review your financial plan regularly?			
Do you know the minimum rate of return required on your investments to ensure you have enough?			

Tax Planning	NOT Important	Important	VERY Important
Are you sure you are currently minimizing unnecessary exposure to tax?			
Are you minimizing personal taxes on non-farm assets such as investments?			
Do you have a strategy in place to minimize the income tax you pay on your investments?			
Are you in a structure that enables you to withdraw funds from your portfolio on a tax-free basis?			

Tax Planning	NOT Important	Important	VERY Important
Does your portfolio give you exposure to underlying securities that produce a mixture of interest, foreign income, Canadian dividends and capital gains, but return on investment is ultimately taxed preferentially as Canadian dividends and/or capital gains?			
Are you maximizing any and all income splitting opportunities available to you, with your spouse or children, or even through a corporate structure or a family trust?			
Do you know which assets can be rolled over tax free to your spouse and which assets will be subject to tax at death?			
Do you know enough about the tax rules regarding the "rollover" of land, equipment and production quota to children and when the rollover can be denied?			
Are you certain about whether the farm rollover will be available for each separate quarter/half/section acreage you own?			
Do you know how much of your lifetime Capital Gains Exemption (CGE) you have left and are you certain which assets are CGE eligible?			
Have you obtained advice about whether you will qualify for the capital gains exemption for each separate quarter/half/section/acreage you own?			
Do you understand how the Principal Residence Exemption (PRE) works if you sell your home located on farmland?			

Tax Planning	NOT Important	Important	VERY Important
If you are a proprietor (not partnership or corporation) do you understand:			
* how to minimize tax exposure on farming income?			
* how a Family Farm Partnership could create tax savings?			
* how incorporating the farm operation could save tax now and in the years leading up to retirement?			
If you operate your farm through a corporation:			
* Are you confident you are minimizing your corporate tax bill?			
* Does your corporate structure ensure that your shares can "roll" to children in the event of your death rather than being taxed?			
* Do you know if your shares will qualify for the lifetime capital gains exemption (CGE)?			
* Does your corporate structure ensure that your shares will always qualify for the lifetime capital gains exemption (CGE) in the event of your death?			
* Have you obtained advice about whether you need a separate holding corporation?			

Tax Planning	NOT Important	Important	VERY Important
* Does your farm succession plan provide for the most tax effective transfer of shares to family members?·			
*` Do you understand how corporately held insurance can create a tax efficient succession plan?			
* Do you know if you are maximizing access to the lowest corporate tax rate?			
Does your current corporate structure:·			
* maximize income splitting opportunities with your family members on an annual basis·			
* on the sale of your business and on your death? (i.e. ability to split income with them through the payment of dividends currently and subsequent to your death and to utilize your capital gains exemption on the potential share sale of your farm)			
If you own shares in a farm corporation, have you obtained advice about whether or not your farm will qualify for the capital gains exemption in the event of a share sale?			

Tax Planning	NOT Important	Important	VERY Important
If you have multiple shareholders in your farm, do you have a shareholders' agreement?			
* If you have a shareholders' agreement, does it provide for a tax efficient exit from your farm on retirement, disagreement, death or disability? ·			
* Does the shareholders' agreement adequately protect your family in the event of your death or does it favour the remaining shareholders? ·			
* Does the shareholders' agreement clearly outline how the value of your shares will be determined on death, disability and retirement?			
Have you reviewed what the tax savings could be by holding any existing personally owned life insurance through your corporation rather than in your personal names?			
Is your corporate structure set up to minimize exposure to your farm's creditors, in particular, if you have significant cash or investment assets inside your corporation(s)?			
Do you have a formal farm succession plan in place?			

ESTATE PLANNING	NOT Important	Important	VERY Important
Do you know:			
* how taxes will affect your estate			
* how much your estate will pay in probate fees			
Do you know how tax will impact your:			
* non-registered investments?			
* registered assets (RRSP's, RRIF's)?			
* other assets such as real estate?			
Do you understand how the farm rollover rules apply at death?			
Do you understand how the capital gains exemption applies at death?			
Have you completed a recent inventory of:			
* assets of significant value?			
* personal effects?			
* tems of emotional value?			
Do you know the difference between "joint tenancy" and "tenancy in common" and the reasons for using the various ownership methods?			
Have you made, or do intend on making gifts during your lifetime?			
Do you have a current Will?			

ESTATE PLANNING	NOT Important	Important	VERY Important
Have you specifically discussed your estate plan with your family?			
Have you specifically discussed your intentions regarding your farm operation with your children?			
Have you obtained advice about ways to create a "fair" distribution of estate value as between farming and non-farming children?			

Do you have any concerns about: ·
 	
  * how your beneficiaries will manage and/or spend their inheritance? ·
 	
  * whether a marriage breakdown could put your child's inheritance at risk? ·
 	
  * how your family will deal with the family cottage?			

Do you know all the uses of trusts and how they can benefit you and your beneficiaries?			
Do you understand how trusts can save income tax?			
Do you understand how trusts can protect your children from marriage breakdown or creditor claims?			

ESTATE PLANNING	NOT Important	Important	VERY Important
Have you selected: 　* an Executor and alternate 　　Executor?· 　* a guardian for minor children?· 　* a Power of Attorney for financial 　　and property matters?· 　* a Power of Attorney for end of life 　　decisions?			
Does your current Will reflect your family's current circumstances and current wishes or does it need to be updated?			
Is your Will drafted to minimize potential family conflict upon your death?			
Have you included long-term trusts in your Will planning for income tax savings for your beneficiaries on their inheritance?			
Does your Will help protect your beneficiaries' inheritances from potential matrimonial and creditor claims? (i.e. Is this a reason to incorporate testamentary trusts?)			
Do you want to be able to control the use and timing of your child's inheritance after your death? (i.e. Is this a reason to incorporate testamentary trusts?)			
If you plan for some but not all of your children to take over your farm, have you devised a plan to treat all children equitably (presuming this is your intention)?			

ESTATE PLANNING	NOT Important	Important	VERY Important
Are you in a second marriage, and if so, does your Will ensure your current spouse and any children from your previous marriage are provided for consistent with your wishes?			

RISK MANAGEMENT	NOT Important	Important	VERY Important
Do you know what the tax liability will be on the second to die of you and your spouse?			
Are there sufficient liquid assets available to fund this liability without forcing the sale of your illiquid assets such as your farm and real estate?			
Have you explored ways to minimize this tax cost on your death? (i.e. either funding with insurance or potentially considering an estate freeze in favour of your children)			
Have you obtained tax advice on potential exposure to U.S. estate tax on your death?			
Do you know if you have too much or too little insurance in place to ensure your family's financial security in the event of your premature death? (i.e. income replacement insurance)			

List below any issues you want to discuss with:

1. Family Members:

_____

_____

_____

2. Partners or Shareholders in Your farming Operation:

_____

_____

_____

3. Your Financial Advisor:

_____

_____

_____

In the following Chapters

I would like to talk about selecting

a good financial or wealth advisor.

Getting this right

means you are well on your way

to preserving and growing your wealth.

CHAPTER 22

WHAT TYPE OF ADVISOR SHOULD I CHOOSE?

Why is this important? Two Main Reasons:

REASON #1

If you hire or are working with a financial advisor who does not take a holistic approach to managing your wealth, you may be working with an advisor who does not see the big financial picture in your life and only will advise within their core competency.

They may shy away from giving you advice or directing you to someone who can give you advice on other areas of your financial life critically important to your financial well-being.

REASON #2

Families may be getting incomplete advice.

If you HIRE or are working with an advisor who does not or cannot offer an integrated approach to managing your wealth, you will need to work with additional advisors to get a complete picture of your overall wealth.

Coordinating the advice from multiple advisors can be a challenge.

When you work with multiple advisors to provide advice on the various aspects of your financial life, you will find that they may not necessarily communicate with each other to get a full understanding of your overall investment strategy and financial goals.

As a result, they may offer conflicting and sometimes incomplete investment, tax, trust, business succession and estate planning advice.

You may be making financial decisions that happen in isolation of your overall investment objectives and financial needs. The result is a collection of investments that are **fragmented, expensive, not very tax-efficient and not doing as well as you expected.**

Aren't All Financial Advisors the Same?

A wide range of differences exist between the expertise and services offered by the various types of financial advisors.

Not knowing what these differences are and hiring the wrong financial advisor can be harmful to your financial health. A financial advisor is a professional who renders financial services to clients. The terms such as financial advisor and financial specialist maybe general terms or job titles used by investment professionals and do not denote any specific designations.

When evaluating investment advisors, selecting the advisor with the lowest fee possible may not always be the most prudent decision.

A wealth advisor or financial planner offering the services of private wealth management can offer a full range of services for the same fee you may already be paying your stock broker or mutual fund advisor.

When the fees charged are embedded (hidden), as they are in many mutual funds, the investor often mistakenly believes the service is free.

When the fee is charged separately or is disclosed, and the investor only receives investment advice, this advice becomes a commodity.

As a result, the only difference between advisors is the size of the advisors' fee.

The best way to evaluate advisors is by asking the 7 questions mentioned in Chapter 13.

To access these questions, **go to:**

www.7keyquestions.ca

You as a smart investor will find it much easier to evaluate their level of service and determine whether their fees match their level of service.

CHAPTER 23

WHAT CAN I EXPECT IN TERMS OF FEES

Advisors are paid for their services in three ways:

1. Commissions
2. Fee-based – Combination of commission and fee only
3. Fee-only

1. Stock brokers and mutual fund salespeople make money when they sell a stock or a fund.

1.1 Stock brokers receive a transaction fee or a flat fee for each stock or bond they put into your account.

1.2 The fees for mutual funds are called loads and are charged:

- when your advisor buys a fund
- when your advisor sells a fund (the full commission is charged if sold in the first year and declines every year thereafter to $0, typically after seven years) or
- on an annual basis (a flat fee based on **Assets Under Management** (AUM)).

2. Fee-based advisors may receive both fees and commissions. They will charge fees based on Assets Under Management (AUM) for their financial/investment planning services and receive commissions for the products they recommend as well.

Total management fees can thus range from 1.50% to as high as 3.5% when you combine both investment advisor fees and mutual fund manager fees.

3. Fee-only advisors are paid directly by their clients and do not receive commissions or fees based on **Assets Under Management.** This fee can be a flat retainer fee or an hourly rate. The hourly or retainer fee can vary widely based on advisor experience and complexity of a client's financial affairs.

Some people ask, "Why should I pay you for the services my commission advisor does for free?"

They believe, incorrectly, that commission advisors are not being paid by the client.

Recall that the advisor is indeed being compensated either by commission or transaction fee for brokers or by having the mutual fund company deduct the fee from the investments or by charging a fee directly.

One important factor to consider is that for the same fee (or commission) that you pay a stock broker or mutual fund representative to buy and sell stocks and funds, you can receive comprehensive, investment and wealth planning from a full-service Wealth Advisor who is backed by an Investment Management Team.

The fee you pay, either embedded or visible, should be based on the value you receive. If the advice given is just pure investment advice, then the fee should be lower.

If the advice includes an investment policy statement, financial planning, retirement planning, estate planning, tax planning or integrated wealth management, the fee should reflect the additional value from the services provided.

A fee-based or fee-only advisor will have access to a wide range of additional services that can add significant value. The fee they charge should reflect the level of services they provide and value you receive from these services.

The Bottom Line?

1. When evaluating investment advisors, selecting the advisor with the lowest fee may not always be the most prudent decision.

2. To get full value for the fees you are paying, you should hire a wealth advisor or financial planner who offers, or has access to, fully integrated investment and wealth management services.

3. Wealth advisors who offer, or have access to, an investment management team will have a disciplined asset allocation process designed specifically for your unique needs.

4. Some wealth advisors offer or have access to private money managers that focus on maximizing your after-tax rate of return. Taxes are probably one of the largest expenditures that you will make over your lifetime.

Check your investment management fees. If you are already paying the standard embedded mutual fund management fee between 2% – 2.75% and are only getting investment advice, you should ask your advisor if they can offer integrated wealth management services.

Integrated Wealth Management

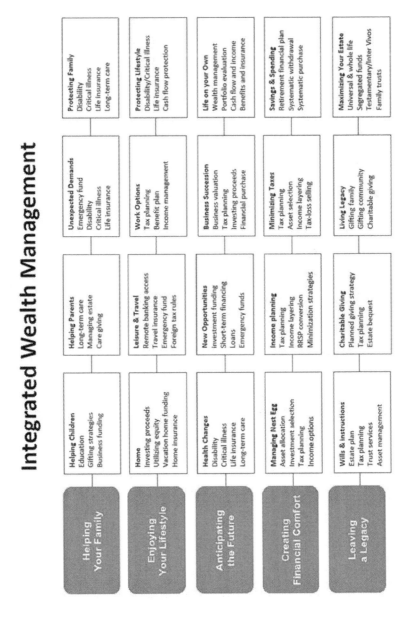

Source Published with Permission: Barry LaValley, President, The Retirement Lifestyle Center

If your advisor is unable to offer these services, you may want to consider the services of a *Wealth Advisor* or financial planner who offers or has access to integrated wealth management services.

In many cases, your overall cost for investment management and wealth planning advice is available to you for the same fee or even less than what you may already be paying your current financial advisor for just their investment advice alone!

CHAPTER 24

WHAT COMPREHENSIVE SERVICES SHOULD MY ADVISOR BE OFFERING?

What you pay a Wealth Advisor will depend on the level of services offered. The fee could be as low as 1.5% for pure investment advice to as high as 2.5% for integrated investment and wealth management advice.

These services should include:

1. Comprehensive Reporting
2. A Personal Investment Plan
3. True Global Portfolio Diversification
4. Portfolio Diversification by Industry

5. Portfolio Diversification by Investment Style: Growth, Value and Alpha

6. Portfolio Tax Deferral on Non-Registered Accounts

7. Portfolio Downside Risk Management

8. Regular Portfolio Rebalancing

9. Dynamic Currency Hedging

10. A Backing of a Professional Portfolio Management Team

11. A Dedicated Investment Management Team Overseeing the Portfolio Managers

12. Custom Portfolio Design

13. Investment Fee Transparency

14. A Financial Plan

15. A Risk Management Plan

16. A Personal Tax Plan

17. A Business / Farm Tax Plan

18. A Business / Farm Succession Plan

19. An Estate Plan

Source: Assante Wealth Management Personal Wealth Management Presentation.

CHAPTER 25

50 WAYS WEALTH ADVISORS BENEFIT THEIR CLIENTS

Wealth advisors build strong relationships and partnerships with their clients by:

1. Being honest with you, appreciating and valuing you.

2. Caring about you and your money more than anyone who does not share your surname.

3. Being someone whom you can trust and get advice from for all your financial matters.

4. Understanding what money means to you and what motivates you.

5. Listening and asking questions to help you identify and articulate your needs, goals and objectives.

6. Working with you to alleviate worries that keep you awake at night.

7. Coaching you to do the things that will help accomplish your goals.

8. Monitoring changes in your life and family situation.

9. Guiding you through difficult periods in the stock market by sharing a historical perspective.

10. Acting as a sounding/discussion board for ideas you are considering.

11. Providing guidance on what course you should take and giving you an objective perspective.

12. Anticipating future changes and proactively working through them with you.

13. Keeping you on track.

Wealth advisors provide customized wealth planning services by:

14. Helping you make important financial-related decisions.

15. Helping organize and prioritize your financial life.

16. Helping you determine where you are at present.

17. Helping you formalize realistic goals and put them in writing.

18. Making specific recommendations to help you meet your goals.

19. Establishing a clear strategy and action plan.

20. Suggesting creative alternatives that you may not have considered.

21. Preparing an investment policy statement for you.

22. Reviewing and recommending life insurance policies to protect your family.

23. Staying up to date on tax law changes.

24. Helping you reduce your taxes by reviewing your tax returns for possible savings.

25. Working with your tax and legal advisors and other professionals to facilitate and coordinate your overall financial plans.

26. Identifying your saving shortfalls.

27. Helping establish your will and estate, retirement and business succession plans.

28. Helping you transfer wealth efficiently to the next generation.

29. Developing and monitoring a strategy for debt reduction.

Wealth advisors construct personalized client portfolios by:

30. Preparing an asset allocation strategy for you to diversify your investments and achieve the best rate of return for your level of risk tolerance.

31. Performing due diligence on money managers and mutual fund managers to ensure appropriate investment recommendations.

32. Staying up to date with changes in the investment world.

33. Reviewing and revising your portfolio as conditions change.

34. Helping consolidate, simplify and improve your investment performance.

35. Monitoring your investments and converting them into income as needed.

36. Helping you establish better planning and record keeping.

37. Exploring and reviewing potential income-splitting and tax-minimization strategies with you.

38. Recommending and completing appropriate tax-loss selling solutions.

39. Repositioning investments to take full advantage of tax rules.

Wealth advisors ensure they offer exceptional service by:

40. Providing full disclosure and transparency on their fees and processes.
41. Proactively keeping in touch with you by providing customized and personalized information.
42. Providing referrals to and liaising with other professionals such as accountants, actuaries, tax lawyers, as needed.
43. Being only a telephone call away to answer financial questions for you.
44. Serving as a human glossary of financial terms such as beta, P/E ratio, and Sharpe ratio.
45. Listening and providing feedback in a way that a magazine or newsletter writer cannot.
46. Helping educate your children and grandchildren about investments and financial concepts.
47. Educating you on retirement, savings and other financial topics.
48. Helping with other non-financial advice.
49. Providing easy-to-read account statements and reports.
50. Holding seminars to educate you on significant and/ or new financial concepts.

CHAPTER 26

CONCLUSION

Conclusion

As you can see if you have gone through this information in detail, managing your financial assets is much more than handing off the decision-making to a financial advisor (stockbroker, mutual fund salesman, insurance salesman or the nice lady at the bank).

It involves understanding all types of financial advisors and which services they offer.

It also means understanding how they are paid for their services (no one works for free).

It also means that you get what you pay for.

Better services will cost more initially, but good advice will save you money, taxes and headaches.

The wealth you accumulate over the years will be professionally managed and provide for your family and charitable interests.

Take the Next Step

Your Family Farm Transition Strategy™ is an exclusive service available to clients of Assante Private Client Managed Portfolios.

If you're like most farmers, you have built up a sizable nest egg.

However, the journey building that nest-egg may have been somewhat haphazard.

You may have multiple investment accounts with multiple advisors.

You have a rough idea of how much you have saved, but it's a challenge collecting all those investment statements to get a clear picture of what you have.

And when you have everything together you still do not have a good handle on how well all your investments are doing, whether you are on track to meeting your retirement goals, or how much you are paying in fees for investment advice.

CHAPTER 27

YOUR OPTIMAL PORTFOLIO SOLUTION

Retire with confidence

Your Optimal Portfolio Solution™

...is a customized portfolio solution designed around your unique needs. It is designed to maximize your investment growth tax efficiently while staying within your comfort zone in up markets as well as protecting your capital in down markets.

No single investment is right for every point in time. A properly constructed portfolio is needed to help smooth out the markets' ups and downs.

Portfolio diversification is the key. By combining different styles of investments, different asset classes and exposure to various geographic regions, your portfolio is positioned to grow to its potential.

The tax effectiveness of your investments is addressed through tax optimization in your investment portfolio and the use of tax-advantaged investment structures. As you know – it's not how much you make that counts, it's what you get to keep that matters!

8 Steps to Creating a Portfolio That Is Right For YOU! ...

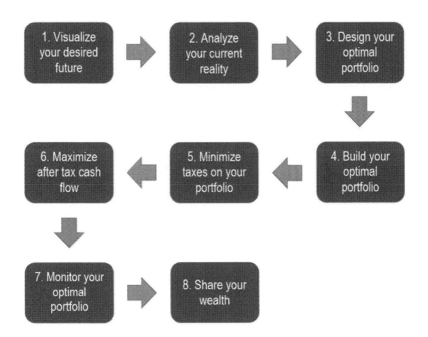

Step 1 - VISUALIZE – your desired future

Your Money Conversation™

1. Visualize your desired future

Our relationship with you begins with us having a conversation with you about your money.

We take the time to really get to know your intimate fears challenges, advantages, excitements, opportunities, lifetime goals and aspirations for you, your family and legacy.

We spend considerable amount of time helping you visualize your need for income, time horizon, risk tolerance, liquidity requirements, growth expectations, income tax characteristics, anticipated changes in your lifestyle and economic variables such as inflation and market volatility.

Result: Vision | Investment: Complimentary

Step 2 - ANALYZE – your current reality

Your Current Reality Audit™

2. Analyze your current reality

Next, we need to know if you are on track to achieving your retirement goals, so before we can begin the process of creating **Your Optimal Portfolio™**, we need to understand your current reality.

This involves exploring all the areas of your personal and family life that have a financial impact on your wealth.

This results in a high-level projection of your net wealth and sufficiency of financial resources needed to help you meet the objectives revealed in **Your Money Conversation™**.

Result: Understanding | Investment: Complimentary

Step 3 - DESIGN – your optimal portfolio

Your Optimal Portfolio Blueprint™

3. Design your optimal portfolio

Before we can build **Your Optimal Portfolio™** you need a blueprint of how your money will be managed.

We begin by creating a document called an Investment Policy Statement (**IPS**). This document captures what we learned about you in **Your Money Conversation™** and **Your Current Reality Audit™**.

The IPS summarizes your needs for:

- Income
- Time horizon
- Risk tolerance
- Liquidity requirements
- Growth expectations

- Income tax characteristics
- Anticipated changes in lifestyle
- Economic variables such as inflation and market volatility

The IPS outlines the strategies the investment management team will employ to build **Your Optimal Portfolio™**. This provides a blueprint of how the team at Assante Private Client, a division of CI Private Counsel LP will manage your investments.

Result:

Personalized Investment Plan | Investment: Complimentary

Step 4 - BUILD – your optimal portfolio

Your Optimal Portfolio™

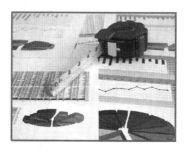

4. Build your optimal portfolio

The next step is to hire the investment management team of Assante Private Client, a division of CI Private Counsel LP to build **Your Optimal Portfolio™** as outlined in **Your Optimal Portfolio Blueprint™.**

Your Optimal Portfolio™ is designed to maximize your investment growth while staying within your comfort zone in up markets as well as protect your capital in down markets.

This is achieved by combining different investment styles, asset classes and exposure to various geographic regions and automatic rebalancing.

Tax efficiency is achieved by the use of tax-advantaged investment structures and appropriate tax planning strategies to minimize overall family tax liability on your investments.

Result:

Your Optimal Portfolio™ | Investment: $250,000

Step 5 - MINIMIZE – taxes on your optimal portfolio

Your Tax Advantaged Solution™

5. Minimize taxes on your portfolio

The more you have the more you pay: it's a fact of life, or is it? Tax planning is an important component of **Your Optimal Portfolio Solution™**, since taxes can have a significant impact on your wealth and eventual legacy.

For your investments held outside of a registered plan, company investment account or trusts, tax efficiency is a critical issue. Since your non-registered assets are not sheltered from taxes, rebalancing transactions and distributions are taxed, adding up to a heavy tax burden.

The tax effectiveness of your investments is addressed through tax optimization of **Your Optimal Portfolio™** and the use of tax-advantaged investment structures to reduce or defer highly taxed interest income and earn tax-efficient dividends or capital gains.

By combining the tax expertise of our wealth planning group and the investment management team, we can create opportunities for deferring, minimizing or eliminating taxes. As you know – it's not how much you make that counts, it's what you get to keep that matters!

Result: More Money| Investment: Complimentary

Step 6 - MAXIMIZE – your after-tax cash flow

Your Tax Efficient Cash Flow Solution™

6. Maximize after tax cash flow

For Retiring Farmers, **Your Tax Efficient Cash Flow Solution™** will allow you to extend the life of **Your Optimal Portfolio™** by allowing you to draw monthly cash flow tax-efficiently, while maintaining potential for growth.

Your Tax Efficient Cash Flow Solution™ returns your original principle first without attracting taxable income in the early years of withdrawal, while deferring the growth in the form of unrealized capital gains.

Since you are not paying taxes on the money returned to you on your original principle, your annual withdrawal is reduced by the amount of taxes you would have otherwise paid.

This extends the life of **Your Optimal Portfolio™** by allowing the tax saved to stay in **Your Optimal Portfolio™** and continue to grow until your original principle has been returned to you.

Once your original principle has been returned to you, you are left with unrealized capital gains in **Your Optimal Portfolio™**. The remaining unrealized gains are returned to you next and are taxed at the capital gains rate which is taxed at ½ your marginal tax rate. Receiving income in the form of capital gains is more efficient than interest income from bank deposits or bonds.

This further extends the life of **Your Optimal Portfolio™** as you only need to withdraw 50% of the tax amount in addition to your monthly income needs.

Result:

Your money lasts longer | Investment: Tailored to your needs

Step 7 - MONITOR – your optimal portfolio

Your Optimal Portfolio Monitor™

7. Monitor your optimal portfolio

Once **Your Optimal Portfolio™** has been implemented, our work is not done.

We meet with you every six to twelve months and more often if necessary to monitor your portfolio and to document any major changes in your personal or financial situation that may require us to make adjustments to **Your Optimal Portfolio™**.

We will also begin work on **Your Family Wealth Foundation™** to help you achieve your lifetime aspirations and ensure you leave a legacy of significance for your family and cherished causes.

Result: Keeping your portfolio optimized | Investment: Tailored to your needs

Step 8 - OPTIMIZE – your wealth

Your Family Wealth Foundation™

8. Share your wealth

Your Family Wealth Foundation™ is where we empower you to simplify your life and optimize your wealth so you can achieve your family's multi-generational goals of wealth accumulation, preservation and distribution.

We work extensively with the Wealth Planning Group of Assante Private Client, a division of CI Private Counsel LP., a team of tax, legal and estate specialists along with your own legal and accounting professionals to consolidate your sophisticated complex financial reality.

We analyze a variety of possible solutions including wealth preservation and tax planning strategies across multiple generations to protect and enhance your wealth.

We explore strategies and solutions that may help you to achieve your family's desired future. The outcome—a legacy of significance for your family and cherished causes.

Result: Your Family Wealth Foundation | Investment: Complimentary

CHAPTER 28

THE SECOND OPINION PORTFOLIO AUDIT™

You may be asking yourself the following questions:

1. Have I saved enough?
2. What is the combined average annual return on all my investments this past year, over the past three, five or ten years?
3. Will these returns help me achieve my goals short term AND long term?
4. Am I comfortable with the risk level of my investments?

5. Can I reduce the tax payable on my investment income?

6. How much am I paying in fees and how are those fees affecting my investment returns?

7. What value am I really getting for the fees I am paying?

Fortunately, I have good news to announce!

"I am offering a **COMPLIMENTARY** Second Opinion Portfolio Audit and Investment Strategy for Families with $250,000 or More in Investable Assets Who Want to Know if Their Investments Are Good Enough to Help Them Reach Their Retirement Goals"

The Second-Opinion Portfolio Audit™ is a technical-sounding name for a simple idea: a detailed analysis of your current portfolio, summarizing all your investments itemizing; the fees, what you are getting for those fees, how well your investments are doing and if your portfolio is structured to minimize taxes and risk.

I will listen to you to discover your personal financial situation, goals, comfort level, risk tolerance and needs. This will help me have a Personalized Investment Strategy* created for you which will allow me to better assess whether your current portfolio is good enough to help you reach your retirement goals. This investment strategy* will outline how your investments should be managed based on your personal situation and is how the investment management team we recommend to our clients would manage your money should you decide to become a client.

Should you decide to accept the recommendations outlined in the Personalized Investment Strategy* and become a client you will also receive a comprehensive Financial Plan and Estate Plan at no additional charge if you have a minimum of $250,000 invested in Evolution Private Managed Accounts and a comprehensive Wealth Plan if you have a minimum of $1,000,000 invested in Private Client Managed Portfolios.

In many cases, your overall cost for investment management and wealth planning advice is available to you for the same fee or even less than what you may already be paying your current financial advisor for just their investment advice alone!

So, What's My Motivation?

My goal is really very straight forward:

- To help you grow your money so that you can achieve financial freedom, security and peace of mind and help you avoid the mistakes my father made.
- To provide you with actionable strategies that you can use to grow your wealth .
- To protect your wealth and help you create a legacy for your family for generations to come.

I am aligned with a team of financial experts that can help me put you on **Your Personal Path to Financial Freedom, Security & Peace of Mind™**.

I am confident that by providing you with a complimentary Personalized Investment Strategy* you will want to become a client.

I believe that it is far easier to show you a sample of what you can expect as a client, rather than make a promise that you can only experience if you become a client.

Some financial advisors make promises but sadly, cannot or do not deliver on those promises.

By showing you what it is like to be one of my clients, I am very confident you will make the decision to become a client.

If after reviewing your **Personalized Investment Strategy**, you decide that you are not ready to become a client, or you do not see the value in what I have provided, or you are extremely happy with your current financial advisor, you are free to keep everything I have provided you, to use with your current financial advisor without charge.

You are welcome to call me anytime during regular business hours. If I am unavailable and you have left a message, I guarantee that I will return your call within 24 hours.

You see, I believe that by providing exceptional value even before you become a client, you will want to become a client.

Are you the right Client?

Often, potential clients like you wonder if our recommended programs are suitable for them.

Here are some ways to know if we can assist you in your wealth creation and preservation.

Are you someone who:

1. is an individual in the 50+ age group with minimum investible assets of $250,000 or more?
2. is looking forward to retirement or has recently retired?
3. has worked hard to reach a secure place where they're able to take care of their family and contribute to their community?
4. would rather spend their time with their family doing the things that are important to their family?
5. realizes that retirement planning is much more than portfolio performance or just about numbers?
6. is ready to establish a long-term plan that will assure them of their family's future security?
7. Doesn't have the desire, expertise, or the extra time to manage their retirement investment portfolio?
8. has decided to consider delegating their financial matters to a skilled, experienced and dependable group of financial planning and investment professionals?
9. is looking for a proactive and personalized service?

I look forward to meeting you to complete...

YOUR Second Opinion Portfolio Audit™

You can contact me Adrian Spitters at:

604.855.6846 – aspitters@assante.com

Or visit

www.secondopinionportfolioaudit.com

Go ahead, call for a personal consultation.

No obligation whatsoever

I want you to be an informed consumer – one who can stare down those imminent threats, and sleep peacefully.

DOWNLOAD MY FREE BOOK

Do you have the right financial advisor working for you? Not sure?

Find out in my new book:

Who's Investing Your Money?

Learn How to Ask the Right Questions to Select the Best Financial Advisor for Your Situation

To get your free book visit:

www.whosinvestingyourmoney.com

Adrian Spitters •

Senior Wealth Advisor •

Assante Capital Management Ltd.

604 - 855 - 6846 •

aspitters@assante.com

Web: www.yourfarmtransitionadvisor.ca

CHAPTER 29

APPENDIX A

ESTATE FREEZE

An Effective Tax Planning Tool to Transfer Farm Assets Tax Efficiently

The following content has been reproduced from the "Estate Freezes" Reference Guide, published by the Wealth Planning Group of Assante Private Client, a division of CI Private Client Counsel LP. Reproduced with permission.

The estate freeze is a strategy used by many Canadian farmers to help accomplish estate planning, farm succession and asset protection objectives.

This reference guide provides a general introduction to estate freezes, outlines the potential benefits and disadvantages associated with these transactions and reviews implementation and structuring considerations.

Introduction

An estate freeze is a mechanism that permits you to lock-in, or freeze, the value of your farm interests at their current value by exchanging them for property having a static value. Future growth can be maintained and also passed to others as a result, which can produce a variety of potential tax and non-tax benefits. You will generally only consider implementing an estate freeze once you have accumulated sufficient wealth to live in your chosen lifestyle for the remainder of your lifetime.

Corporations are often used to facilitate the property exchanges involved in estate freezes. For example, transferring growth assets to a farm corporation in exchange for preference shares having a fixed value (sometimes referred to as freeze shares) is an effective way of capping your exposure to future growth. Entitlement to future growth will then pass to holders of new shares (common shares) issued as part of the estate freeze, instead of to you.

You would determine who would benefit from post-freeze growth, by deciding who will receive new common shares. Your decision would usually be based on a number of factors, including the relative financial position of the persons involved and your objectives for implementing the freeze. For example, if you did not anticipate a need to access future growth, common shares could be issued exclusively to others (such as your spouse, children or other family members). Conversely, if you anticipated occasional future cash flow shortfalls, you might also arrange for some new common shares to be issued to you personally. This is sometimes referred to as a partial freeze. Many factors affect the ultimate structuring of post-freeze shareholdings, including whether or not income-splitting is an objective of the estate freeze, tax and family law considerations and other factors.

Common shares issued as part of an estate freeze generally have a nominal initial value because the corporation's entire value is reflected in the freeze shares. This can allow new individuals to become equity participants in a corporation at minimal cost, which is often a key objective of farmers planning to transfer their farm to next-generation family members, or non-family members such as key employees.

Benefits

The specific benefits that you will derive from implementing an estate freeze depend on a number of factors. Possible benefits include:

➢ minimizing income and probate taxes on death
➢ creating income splitting opportunities
➢ facilitating capital gains exemption planning
➢ facilitating farm succession
➢ allowing control following retirement.

MINIMIZING INCOME AND PROBATE TAXES ON DEATH

Unlike the United States, Canada does not levy death taxes, per se. Nevertheless, Canadians can face significant income tax consequences when they die, due to tax rules that deem individuals to dispose of their assets immediately before death.[6]

These rules result in the recognition and taxation, on death, of capital gains that have accrued throughout your lifetime.[7]

Since these rules apply to untaxed growth in the value of private corporation shares, successful farmers require careful estate planning in order to avoid substantial taxation on death. Estate freeze transactions are often employed to help manage this potential tax liability.

As described estate freezes transfer future growth to others designated by you (referred to as freeze beneficiaries). This results in a transfer of the responsibility to pay tax on that growth to the freeze beneficiaries, creating a tax deferral. Instead of the tax liability being triggered on your death, it is delayed until the freeze beneficiaries die or otherwise dispose of the shares. In the classic estate freeze scenario where next generation family members are named as the freeze beneficiaries, the tax can be deferred over a potentially significant period of time.

---

[6] The dispositions are deemed to occur at fair market value except, most notably, where a deceased transfers his or her capital property to a spouse (or to a qualifying spousal trust). In these situations, the deemed disposition at fair market value will not apply and tax is deferred until the death of the surviving spouse (or until the spouse or spousal trust otherwise disposes of the property).

[7] This date-of-death tax liability can be mitigated where property qualifies for the capital gains exemption.

Deferring tax is valuable since it is generally better to pay taxes later rather than sooner, particularly where lower income tax rates are anticipated in the future. The deferral value of an estate freeze includes both minimizing your date-of-death tax liability and increasing the net wealth of your estate freeze beneficiaries.

Estate freezes can also limit exposure to probate fees, which are a provincial tax imposed when courts process wills. Probate fees are usually applied according to an estate's value: as the value of an estate increases, so do applicable probate fees. Implementing an estate freeze to fix the value of your corporate interests limits exposure to future probate fees in the same way that it minimizes exposure to income tax on death - by preventing future growth from accruing to you.

Note, more generally, that undertaking an estate freeze helps identify and quantify income taxes and probate fees that will likely arise on death. Once determined, you can plan how best to deal with these liabilities within an overall estate plan, which might involve systematically redeeming your freeze shares or implementing life insurance strategies, alternative will arrangements and other solutions.

CREATING INCOME SPLITTING OPPORTUNITIES

Splitting income by using family members' lowest marginal brackets to the fullest extent possible can reduce tax applicable to a family unit and can serve as a method of transferring wealth to the next generation. Facilitating income splitting is often a primary motivation for implementing an estate freeze.

Income splitting can be facilitated where, as part of an estate freeze, new shares are issued to other family members directly or indirectly through a family trust. Dividends could then be declared on the shares held by one or more freeze beneficiaries to the possible exclusion of others (as determined by you as director), effectively splitting the income that you would have otherwise received and been taxed upon. If the other family members are in a lower tax bracket, this could save income tax.

Children and other family members could be beneficiaries of a trust to which new common shares are issued (subject to the attribution rules discussed below). The appropriateness of using a trust depends on your circumstances.

A trust could be appropriate where you:

➢ wish to maintain control over new growth shares

➢ have concerns about children's creditors or potential marital or family property claims

➢ wish to defer the decision as to which children or other family members will receive growth shares and in what proportions

➢ are uncomfortable with children or other family members being involved in current farm affairs.

ATTRIBUTION RULES

The purpose of the attribution rules in the Income Tax Act is to prevent spouses from splitting income and capital gains with each other and parents from splitting income with children. The rules can apply where you transfer property to a spouse or to a relative under the age of 18, or retain too much control over a family trust created as part of an estate freeze. If applicable, income and/or capital gains from the assets are attributed back to you for tax purposes, preventing income splitting and the ability to minimize capital gains tax.

Corporate attribution is an attribution rule that must be considered when implementing estate freezes, since it can apply where the property is transferred to a corporation for the benefit of a spouse or minor relative. If applicable, the rule deems you to receive an annual income inclusion, at a prescribed rate.

Corporate attribution can sometimes be avoided, most notably where your corporation satisfies the small business corporation (SBC) definition. This requires (among other things) that all or substantially all[8] of the corporation's assets are used in an active farm business in Canada. Corporate attribution could still apply if your corporation fell offside of the SBC definition at any time following an estate freeze.

Another way to avoid corporate attribution, if using a family trust, is to ensure that the trust restricts your spouse and any related person, niece or nephew under the age of 18 from being entitled to receive any trust income or capital during your lifetime.

Complex considerations are involved when structuring an estate freeze to avoid the attribution rules, for which professional advice is required.

[8] The Canada Revenue Agency (CRA) interprets this to mean 90%, although the Courts have held that in certain situations it may be less. Please see our reference guide on tax planning for the sale of your business for a detailed discussion of the SBC definition.

Note that it is no longer possible to split income through dividend payments to minor children, grandchildren, nieces or nephews, due to the income splitting tax (often called the kiddie tax). This rule taxes private corporation dividends received by a minor child at the highest marginal rate, eliminating any income-splitting benefit. However, such income splitting is still possible with adult relatives.

FACILITATING CAPITAL GAINS EXEMPTION PLANNING

The capital gains exemption can be used to shelter from tax up to approximately $824,000 of capital gains arising from the sale (or deemed sale on death) of qualifying small business corporation (QSBC) shares.[9] Spouses and individual family members with an ownership position in the farm and farm assets arising from the sale (or deemed sale on death) of shares of a farm corporation or qualifying farm property qualify for up to $1,000,000 each.

Using the capital gains exemption is a key estate-planning objective for farmers, and estate freezes are often used as a component of such planning.

[9] To meet the QSBC definition, shares must satisfy various tests, including regarding the proportion of the corporation's assets that are active business-use assets versus passive non-business use assets. Details are further discussed in our reference guide on tax planning for the sale of your business.

For example, implementing an estate freeze can allow you to access the separate QSBC share exemptions of other family members.

This can result in significant planning opportunities if, in the future, you are contemplating selling qualifying shares for proceeds that will exceed your personal capital gains exemption limit.

Depending on your circumstances, you might also consider crystallizing your QSBC share exemption as part of an estate freeze transaction, if you suspect that the exemption will be repealed in the future or if your shares currently qualify as QSBC shares, but you are concerned that they will not, going forward. If properly implemented, a crystallization transaction steps up the cost base of your shares (to the extent elected) on a tax-free basis.

Strict technical requirements must be met in order for the QSBC share exemption to apply. Unanticipated negative tax consequences can arise if careful planning is not undertaken, particularly in non-arm's length share sale transactions. If in the future, you are considering claiming the exemption in connection with your private corporation shares, you should consult with your professional advisors well in advance to ensure that all technical requirements are satisfied.

FACILITATING FARM SUCCESSION

As retirement approaches, owners start planning for farm succession. In some cases, children will step in to carry on farming, while in others they will not. Alternatively, some children, but not all, will become involved.

Estate freezes are often used to facilitate transfers of farm operations to the next generation. For example, if you wish to limit the financial barriers that your child or children might face to enter the family farm, an estate freeze might be appropriate as it could facilitate new family members becoming equity participants at nominal subscription prices. Incorporating trusts into an estate freeze can permit succession objectives to be met as they develop over time and provide maximum flexibility to farm succession planning, due to their inherent flexibility.

ALLOWING CONTROL FOLLOWING RETIREMENT

Many farmers reach a stage where they are ready to step away from actively running their farm but are averse to relinquishing control, due to emotional and financial ties. For some, maintaining control offers peace of mind where questions exist as to the business acumen of family members taking over the farm. Estate freezes can be structured to allow you to back away from daily farm operations while retaining a desired level of control.

One method of doing so is to issue control shares (voting preferred shares) to yourself as part of an estate freeze. This will not impair the objective of passing future growth entitlement to freeze beneficiaries, yet it satisfies the objective of not foregoing ultimate control over your farm operations. Control shares are typically issued for nominal value. It is recommended that they form a different class of shares than the freeze shares, which separates your voting rights and equity value, creating added flexibility for future planning.

Implementing an estate freeze does not preclude you from continuing as a director and/or officer of a corporation, which can serve as another method of maintaining a voice in the direction and/or management of the farm following retirement from active duty.

Disadvantages

Some potential disadvantages must also be considered when determining whether an estate freeze is appropriate for you.

For example, professional costs will be incurred, both at implementation time and annually to meet tax-reporting obligations. The fees will generally vary depending on the complexity of your farm business affairs and current organizational structure. Before proceeding, your professional advisors should provide you with an outline of the costs that you can reasonably expect to incur.

There is also a frequent concern that implementing an estate freeze poses a risk to your future financial sufficiency. Careful planning is necessary to protect against undertaking a freeze transaction too early, before you reach a sufficient level of wealth. As well, consideration should be given to the range of pre-implementation strategies that can facilitate a freeze being reversed in the future, if necessary (see the related discussion below entitled "can I reverse an estate freeze?").

Loss of control over farm operations is also a common objection to proceeding with an estate freeze. As earlier described, some options exist to mitigate the amount of control that you will forego by freezing your farm interests, which can help alleviate this concern.

Implementation

WHEN SHOULD I CONSIDER IMPLEMENTING AN ESTATE FREEZE?

Determining when to implement an estate freeze requires consideration of your financial position as well as your estate planning and farm succession objectives.

For example, if you are just starting out farming, you are unlikely to implement an estate freeze strictly for the purpose of divesting yourself of anticipated future growth, as it is improbable that you are in a financial position or stage of life to do so. Rather, you would use an estate freeze to cap your farm interests once you have reached a comfortable level of personal wealth and, perhaps, a certain age.

However, a reorganization and partial estate freeze might still be warranted in your circumstances for the income-splitting benefits that it could provide. The decision would depend on your profit projections and family situation, together with the relative income levels of your family members and other considerations.

Market forces and valuation considerations can also affect the determination of when to implement an estate freeze. For example, if you are considering an estate freeze you should be aware of short-term farm business cycle forecasts and projections. If your objective is to minimize income and probate taxes, timing an estate freeze to occur when your farm' value is depressed could result in additional growth being passed along to the beneficiaries of the freeze, further minimizing your exposure to taxes on death.

CAN I REVERSE AN ESTATE FREEZE?

Farmers sometimes wish to reverse an estate freeze that has already been implemented, including when:

➢ unanticipated cash flow constraints arise in retirement

➢ conflicts develop with freeze beneficiaries

➢ other unanticipated post-freeze changes in family or financial situations occur

➢ misunderstandings exist as to the legal nature of the estate freeze (i.e. that the right to future growth was legally transferred to the freeze beneficiaries)

➢ the value of the corporation has decreased, and the value of the freeze shares is no longer reflected in the corporation's current fair market value, which on death could have significant tax implications.

Implementing an estate freeze should generally be considered permanent and, as a result, should only proceed following careful consideration. That being said, there are certain planning measures that can help alleviate unanticipated future difficulties and which may allow for an estate freeze structure to be reversed or thawed, if proper planning is undertaken.

For example, if you anticipate sporadic future cash flow difficulties when planning an estate freeze, you should consider making advance arrangements for salary or bonus continuation following the freeze. Any such salary or bonus would have to be reasonable, in light of services you provide in the future, and must be considered in light of all other planning steps being undertaken (such as paying you a retiring allowance on your retirement, for example, which would be inconsistent with a decision to pay you an ongoing salary).

You should also canvass with freeze beneficiaries the corporation's post-freeze dividend policy, as dividends paid to you on your freeze shares will assist you with retirement cash flow needs. Maintaining a position as a director can help to ensure that you have a level of control over the payment of dividends, as can arranging for nominal-value voting control shares to be issued to you as part of the freeze transaction, as described above.

A **Unanimous Shareholders' Agreement** (USA) is a form of shareholders' agreement that is signed by all shareholders of a corporation and by the corporation itself. A USA, which is binding on the corporation, can override a corporation's articles by restricting certain powers typically exercised by directors and stipulating that they are instead to be exercised by the shareholders.

As a precautionary measure, you might consider entering into a USA with the freeze beneficiaries that includes a clause requiring another freeze to be undertaken if requested in the future by you. The USA would stipulate that the refreeze would be for your benefit. To protect you, this kind of agreement should be signed immediately before implementing an estate freeze, to prevent shareholders from changing their views on the merits of entering into the agreement.

Other, more exotic structuring alternatives exist that can allow for pre-planned unfreezes, including the use of conversion rights and other complex corporate law arrangements. Your professional advisor should be consulted regarding these possibilities when exploring estate freeze structuring options.

WILL I TRIGGER TAX CONSEQUENCES WHEN IMPLEMENTING AN ESTATE FREEZE?

The possibility of inadvertently triggering income tax consequences is a concern whenever property is transferred. Estate freezes typically involve transfers of property that have appreciated in value, and this creates a risk that inherent capital gains could be subject to tax immediately upon implementation. However, estate freezes are routinely structured to comply with special rules, allowing owners who implement properly structured estate freezes to avoid triggering immediate income tax consequences.

As described above, tax that would otherwise apply, is not eliminated; instead, these transactions are permitted to take place on a tax-deferred basis, delaying the application of tax until a future point in time (such as the next disposition of the property, for example).

There are several different rules that can defer tax that would otherwise apply to estate freezes, allowing for some flexibility when structuring these transactions. Planning alternatives will depend on your current structure and should be reviewed with your professional advisors.

Note that the CRA has established administrative

guidelines that, in their view, must also be satisfied for an estate freeze to be a tax-deferred transaction.

In particular, the CRA requires that freeze shares have the following rights and attributes:

> ➤ Freeze shares must be retractable. This means that they must be redeemable at the option of the shareholder.

> ➤ Freeze shares must have a priority right to receive assets when the corporation is dissolved or wound-up.

> ➤ Freeze shares must be transferable without restriction, except for those imposed under corporate law.

> ➤ Freeze shares must have sufficient voting rights to protect against changes to the rights and attributes listed above.

> ➤ The corporation must be restricted from paying dividends on other share classes that will impair the corporation's ability to redeem the freeze shares.

Conclusion

An estate freeze may provide significant tax and non-tax benefits for you and your family members if, for example, you have achieved a sufficient level of wealth to live in your chosen lifestyle throughout the balance of your lifetime or if you can take advantage of opportunities to split income.

However, the tax benefits that might be achieved must be considered together with the potential consequences to your farm operations, your personal financial sufficiency and your estate planning and farm succession objectives. The preceding discussion is intended to outline many of the points that you should canvass with your professional advisors when reviewing the possibility of an estate freeze.

CHAPTER 30

APPENDIX B

FAMILY TRUSTS

An Effective Way to Protect Family Assets

The following content has been reproduced from the "Family Trusts" Reference Guide, published by the Wealth Planning Group of Assante Private Client, a division of CI Private Client Counsel LP. Reproduced with permission.

Family trusts continue to be a legitimate and valuable planning tool that can be very effective in providing solutions to succession planning and addressing various concerns such as tax reduction and asset protection from commercial liabilities and creditors.

The key to successfully using family trusts is understanding how they work, and how they can most effectively fit into an estate plan.

What is a family trust?

A trust is an obligation that binds a person or persons (the trustee(s)) to deal with certain property (the trust property) for the benefit of specified persons (the beneficiaries). In simple terms, a trust is basically a relationship between trustees and beneficiaries.

To create a trust, a person, referred to as a settlor, transfers legal ownership of property to the trustee(s), and provides instructions to the trustee(s) regarding how the property is to be used for the benefit of the beneficiaries.

A commonly-used trust arrangement is a testamentary trust – that is, one made in a will which takes effect only on the death of the person who made the will. (Further information on testamentary trusts can be found in our reference guide on testamentary trusts.) Trust arrangements can also be made in a trust agreement that is to take effect during a lifetime, and these are referred to as lifetime trusts or by the Latin term inter vivos trusts.

A family trust is simply a form of lifetime trust established for the benefit of a particular family or for certain members of that family.

How can family trusts be used?

One of the most valuable features of trusts is their flexibility. For example, in creating a trust, there is considerable flexibility about matters such as the selection of beneficiaries, how the beneficiaries are to benefit and the ongoing investment and management of trust assets. Other features of trusts include:

> ➢ the ability to provide for successive beneficiaries
> ➢ the ability to place a wide variety of assets into a trust
> ➢ the ability to maintain privacy, and
> ➢ the unique tax rules that apply to trusts.

These features combine to make trusts an effective way to meet a wide range of objectives. Family trusts, for example, can be used for both tax and non-tax purposes, as the following illustrations demonstrate:

➢ Family trusts work well for the owner/manager of a farm who would like to split income with a spouse and adult children with low incomes (for example, university students) in order to achieve tax efficiencies. Note that all references to a spouse in this reference guide apply equally to common-law partners.

➢ For those who own significant investment assets or have an investment corporation, family trusts can be used to split income from the investment assets or corporation among adult children.

➢ For a farmer with children who may or may not be interested in becoming active shareholders, family trusts can be a very useful succession-planning tool, providing a vehicle for ongoing management and control of the farm.

➢ A family trust can be an effective way to provide for a former spouse and/or children of a previous marriage.

➢ For someone who is concerned about possible financial difficulties in the future, a family trust can help to provide financial security for his or her family.

➤ A family trust might be a tax-effective vehicle for providing for elderly parents or other adult relatives who require financial support.

How are family trusts taxed?

For income tax purposes, a trust is considered to be a separate taxpayer and is therefore required to file annual income tax returns. In filing these returns, the trust can deduct income and capital gains that are paid or payable to its beneficiaries during the year (as discussed below) – and the beneficiaries must then include these amounts in filing their tax returns.

Dividends and capital gains received by a trust retain their identity when paid out to the beneficiaries. For example, capital gains received by a trust and paid to a beneficiary will continue to be considered capital gains in the hands of the beneficiary for income tax purposes, so only 50% of the capital gain received by the beneficiary would be taxable. Similarly, a dividend received by a trust and distributed to a beneficiary would retain its character as a dividend and would be taxed as a dividend in the hands of the beneficiary. This is an attractive feature of trusts, as it provides the opportunity for creativity and flexibility in making distributions to beneficiaries.

All of the taxable income of a family trust is taxed at the highest marginal tax bracket in the province in which the trust is a resident. Trusts are also not allowed to claim personal tax credits such as the personal credit and the age credit. Because of these rules, the trustees of a family trust typically ensure that all income and capital gains earned by the family trust are paid or made payable to the beneficiaries, to be taxed in the hands of the beneficiaries (subject to the attribution rules outlined below).

There are numerous provisions in the Income Tax Act that restrict or limit the tax benefits of using a trust. For example:

> ➤ To prevent the indefinite deferral of tax on capital gains through the use of a trust, a trust is treated as having disposed of its capital property at fair market value every 21 years. This 21-year rule could trigger a taxable capital gain (or loss). A large gain could, therefore, result in a significant tax bill for the trust every 21 years.

➤ To reduce income-splitting among family members, there are attribution rules that can cause income, losses and capital gains from property transferred to a trust to be taxed in the hands of the individual who transferred the property. In the case of trusts, these rules will apply in the following situations:

- if there is any possibility of the transferred property reverting to the individual

- if the individual can exercise some control over the property

- with respect to income from property transferred through a trust to or for the benefit of a related minor beneficiary (such as a child, grandchild, niece or nephew), and

- with respect to income and capital gains from property transferred through a trust to or for the benefit of the individual's spouse.

There are, however, certain exceptions to the attribution rules. For example:

- The attribution rules do not apply to adult beneficiaries (e.g. adult children or adult grand-children) in most circumstances. A beneficiary is considered an adult as of the year in which he or she turns 18.

- The attribution rules do not apply to capital gains earned on assets transferred either directly to minor children or grandchildren or to a trust for the benefit of minor children or grandchildren.

- A special kiddie tax is imposed on dividends from private corporations and certain other income passed through a trust to persons under 18 years old. This effectively eliminates any tax benefits of splitting income with minor children or minor grandchildren through a family trust.

A family trust must, therefore, be designed with these tax rules in mind.

AMOUNT PAID OR PAYABLE

As indicated above, in computing its income (including capital gains) for a particular year, a trust is allowed a deduction for all amounts which are paid or made payable to a beneficiary in the year. The beneficiary would then report these amounts on his or her tax return for the year, subject to the attribution rules described earlier. For these purposes, an amount is only considered payable in a year if it is paid to a beneficiary or if the beneficiary is entitled to enforce its payment in the year.

The current position of the Canada Revenue Agency (CRA) is that expenditure may be considered paid or payable, and therefore deductible by a trust, if it was made for the beneficiary's benefit. This may include an amount paid out of the trust for the support, maintenance, care, education, enjoyment and advancement of the beneficiary, including the beneficiary's necessities of life. For example, it may be acceptable for the trust to pay third parties or to reimburse the parents for specific expenses attributable to the children (or grandchildren) such as clothing, tuition, day or summer camp, day care, airline tickets (for the children or grandchildren), sports lessons and equipment, computers, furniture (for a child's or grandchild's room), music lessons and music equipment, and gifts. The key is to maintain proper documentation and to be able to demonstrate that the money was used for the benefit of the beneficiary.

How is a family trust established?

In very general terms, a family trust, like any other trust, is established by the transfer of certain assets to one or more trustees, along with directions to the trustee(s) regarding how the assets are to be managed and how the named beneficiaries are to benefit. This is all typically set out in a trust agreement (sometimes referred to as a trust deed or trust indenture).

To ensure the validity of the trust for tax and legal purposes, there are certain requirements that must be met. In addition, the income tax implications of the transfer of the assets to the trust must be fully considered. It is therefore extremely important to involve well-qualified professionals in the planning and establishment of a family trust. Some of the issues that must be dealt with in setting up a family trust are outlined below.

THE TRANSFER OF ASSETS

Depending on the purpose for which the family trust is being created, the initial transfer of assets to the family trust may be made by different individuals. The income tax implications must also be considered. For example:

➤ Where a family trust is created in the context of an estate freeze, a grandparent or family friend might establish a family trust using a gold coin; alternatively, a cash gift (for example, a gift of $500) could be made, which would be used to purchase a coin for the trust and to pay the trust's expenses. Having a grandparent or family friend as initial contributors to the trust would often avoid the potential application of the attribution rules referred to earlier. Further assets would then be acquired by the family trust.

➤ In the case of a family trust created for income-splitting purposes, an individual who owns considerable assets could establish the family trust by transferring the ownership of the assets to the trustees. (An alternative would be to simply give assets to family members directly, but this would eliminate the ability to take advantage of the benefits that a family trust can provide.)

As noted earlier, a wide variety of assets can be held by trusts, including real estate, cash, a portfolio of securities such as shares, bonds and mutual funds, and shares of privately held corporations. It should be noted, however, that for tax purposes, a transfer of assets to a family trust (or to family members directly) is treated as a sale of the assets at their fair market value as at the time of the transfer. Accordingly, any accumulated gains in the transferred assets would be taxable to the transferring individual in the year the transfer was made. Because of this, it is often best to transfer assets with a cost base, for tax purposes, that is approximately equal to the value of the assets. Alternatively, cash could be gifted to the trust. Registered assets should not be used for this purpose because of the tax liability that would be triggered by the withdrawal from the registered plan.

THE TRUSTEES

There are a number of factors, both tax-related and non-tax-related, that should be considered in selecting the trustees of the family trust.

Given the often long-term nature of a family trust, the

trustees selected should be willing and able to act, and should have the necessary knowledge and ability to be able to handle the assets to be held in the trust as well as all of the other obligations required of trustees. A mechanism should also be included for the appointment of replacement trustees in case the trustees named are unwilling or unable to act or to continue to act.

While an individual who transfers assets to a family trust may be a trustee of the trust if desired, he or she should not be the sole trustee and should not be in a position to control the distribution of the income and capital of the trust. As noted above, if that control is maintained, then any income or capital gains earned by the family trust will be taxed in the hands of the transferring individual, which would defeat an important benefit of the family trust.

Another important factor to consider in selecting the trustees of a family trust is the residence of the trustees. In general, for income tax purposes, a trust is considered to be resident in the jurisdiction in which the majority of the controlling trustees reside. As significant unintended tax consequences, could result if the residence of trustees causes a family trust to be a non-resident of Canada for tax purposes, you should seek advice if you are considering naming an individual who lives in a foreign country as a trustee.

THE BENEFICIARIES

The trust document names or identifies which family members are to be potential beneficiaries of the family trust. For example, adult children and grandchildren are often named as beneficiaries. The beneficiaries could also include any future grandchildren, and, if desired, present or future spouses or common-law partners of children and grandchildren.

Corporations are also often included as a beneficiary of the family trust. A corporate beneficiary may be owned by one or more of the beneficiaries of the family trust.

The individual who establishes the trust or transfers assets to the trust may or may not be named a beneficiary, depending on the reasons for the establishment of the family trust. To avoid the application of the attribution rules, that individual should at most be named only as a possible income beneficiary, and not a capital beneficiary. Careful tax and legal planning is necessary in selecting trust beneficiaries.

PAYMENTS OF INCOME AND CAPITAL

In most cases, a family trust gives the trustees complete discretion to decide whether, how much and to whom income and capital are to be distributed in any year. This allows for maximum flexibility, so that the trustees can decide each year, based on current circumstances, what amount, if any, of the income and/or capital is to be paid to the beneficiaries, and in what proportions.

However, as noted above, care must be taken to ensure that the individual who transfers assets to the family trust cannot in any way obtain any of the capital of the trust.

Note that for tax purposes, capital gains are treated as income. Under trust law, however, capital gains are considered to be capital, so that the trustees could only distribute these to capital beneficiaries of the trust. If desired, however, the trust document can define what is to constitute income of the trust for trust purposes. Accordingly, depending on the particular objectives of the trust, the income of the trust could be defined to include capital gains. This would make the treatment of these amounts the same for both trust and tax purposes and could also facilitate desired distributions to beneficiaries.

What are the tax benefits of a family trust?

Despite what may seem to be onerous tax rules relating to trusts, there are still tax benefits to be gained by using a family trust. For example, in certain situations:

➢ A family trust can allow the income generated by investment assets or by a family farm (generally one that is incorporated) to be split among adult family members to achieve tax savings if family members are in lower tax brackets. Capital gains may also be split among family members.

➢ A family trust can be used as a means of transferring the growth in value of a family farm to the next generation on a tax-deferred basis.

➢ A family trust can be used to assist in asset protection along with purification of passive assets before the sale of the family farm.

In addition to these tax saving opportunities, family trusts also save on probate fees, which run as high as 1.5% in some provinces. This is because property held in a family trust would not form part of the estate of the individual who transferred the property to the trust and would therefore not be subject to probate fees.

How are the tax benefits achieved?

The tax benefits of a family trust arise in different ways, depending on the family situation and on the primary objectives of the trust. The following examples illustrate how a family trust can be used to achieve tax savings.

EXAMPLE #1

Owner/Manager Incorporated Family Farm

Here is a general outline of the steps involved in using a family trust to save on taxes in the case of an owner/manager of an incorporated family farm:

➢ The family trust would be created in the manner noted above, with the owner/manager usually named as one of two or more trustees. Other trustees could include friends or extended family, but a majority of the trustees should not also be beneficiaries.

➢ The existing shareholders of the incorporated family farm would exchange their common shares in the corporation for new shares of a different class. These new shares are usually preferred shares that have a fixed redemption price (based on the value of the original common shares), as well as a fixed maximum rate of return. Control is usually retained by the existing shareholders.

➤ The family trust would then subscribe for new common shares of the corporation for a nominal subscription (or purchase) price. Typically, the family trust borrows the necessary funds from a bank or other third party, and later repays the loan once it receives a dividend from the corporation.

The result of these arrangements is that the family trust becomes the owner of the common shares of the incorporated family farm.

As the owner:

➤ The family trust would benefit from the future growth in the value of the farm.

➤ The family trust would also receive dividends on the shares it owns. These would be paid to it out of the active farm income earned by the incorporated farm.

The tax benefits of this arrangement would be achieved as follows:

➢ The family trust would pay the dividends it receives from the incorporated family farm to the beneficiaries of the trust, who would typically be lower-income family members.

➢ Because dividends paid out of the trust to beneficiaries retain their identity (as described earlier), the dividends would qualify for the dividend tax credit, a special tax credit available for taxable dividends from Canadian corporations. The effect of this tax credit is that an adult beneficiary of the family trust with no other income could receive significant non-eligible dividend income through the trust each year and not pay any tax on this income.

In this way, having a family trust as a shareholder of a corporation managing an active farming business effectively allows expenses for an adult child, such as education or travel expenses, to be paid with income that is taxed at the corporate level on active farming income, instead of being taxed at the parent's personal tax rate if they would have received the income directly as a salary or bonus.

- Another strategy, in the owner/manager incorporated family farm scenario, is the use of a corporate beneficiary. In situations where family members are not in a low tax bracket in a particular year, or family members are too young to receive distributions from the family trust, the introduction of a corporate beneficiary can defer the tax burden.

- Any profits of the owner/manager incorporated family farm could be paid to the family trust as a dividend and then allocated to the corporate beneficiary. As dividends between two connected taxable Canadian corporations flow tax-free, the tax is deferred.

- The use of a corporate beneficiary could also assist with the owner/manager incorporated family farm in eliminating any excess cash not deemed necessary in the day-to-day operations of the farm. The elimination of the excess cash could help enable the farm corporation to qualify for the capital gains exemption in the event of a sale, provide asset protection and allow for tax planning on the eventual distribution of the funds.

EXAMPLE #2

Investment Corporation

Similar potential tax savings can be achieved by using a family trust in the case of an investment corporation. If the dividend income from the investment corporation flows through the family trust and is distributed to an adult beneficiary who has no other income, a family could again save significant amounts of income tax.

Over time (and subject to the 21-year rule mentioned earlier), as the family trust's shares in the farm or investment corporation grow in value, the trustees of the family trust can distribute the shares to Canadian resident children at an appropriate time (for example, on the death or retirement of the parent). This distribution can be on a tax-deferred basis, so that the taxes on any capital gains accrued on the shares up to that time are deferred until the child disposes of the shares. Without the family trust, the capital gains would have continued to accrue in the parent's hands and would be taxable on the death of the surviving parent. The family trust, therefore, allows for a potentially longer, inter-generational deferral of this income tax liability.

EXAMPLE #3

Investment Assets

A family trust can also be used to achieve tax savings even where there is no farm or corporation involved. Here is an example of how this could be achieved:

- ➤ A parent or grandparent in the highest tax bracket could place investment assets into a family trust for the benefit of one or more adult children and/or adult grandchildren who are in lower tax brackets. As noted earlier, it would be desirable to use either cash or assets with a high-cost base so that no gains are triggered on the transfer of the assets. Also, these assets should be surplus assets – that is, the parent or grandparent should not require these assets for his or her needs.

- ➤ The income earned by the trust on the investments would then be paid or made payable to the children or grandchildren, where it would be taxed at their lower rate.

This can be a very tax-effective way for a parent or grandparent to provide financial assistance to lower income adult family members.

What are the non-tax benefits of a family trust?

FARM SUCCESSION

In the case of an incorporated family farm, family trusts can also be used to provide for the smooth succession of the farm from one generation to the next. In this case, the trustees of the family trust could hold the shares of the corporation for the benefit of the entire family until details regarding the succession of the farm have been determined. This is particularly important where, for example, it is uncertain whether, or which, children will participate in the family farm. The family trust provides the flexibility to determine which children will participate as shareholders, and in what proportions the trust's holdings in the family farm and the trust's income will be divided.

PROTECTION FROM CREDITORS

Family trusts can also help to protect assets from possible future creditors. If all distributions of income and capital are at the discretion of the trustees, the beneficiaries' creditors should not be able to seize any of the family trust's assets.

In addition, under an appropriately established family trust, the use of a family trust may help to provide some protection of assets from future marital or family property claims involving a beneficiary. It should be noted, however, that as a result of several court cases, protection from marital or family property claims by the use of a trust may not be quite as certain as protection from other creditors.

PROVIDING FOR FINANCIALLY DEPENDENT ADULT BENEFICIARIES OR THOSE WITH SPECIAL NEEDS

If an individual is providing financial support for an adult relative, such as elderly parents or a child or sibling with special needs, a family trust can be an effective way to provide for their ongoing financial needs.

Note that in the case of special needs adults, there are special considerations in planning and establishing a trust for their benefit. For example, the trust document must be carefully drafted where there is a desire to ensure that social assistance payments that special needs adults are typically eligible to receive will not be adversely affected. In addition, where a trust beneficiary is eligible to claim the disability tax credit (due to mental or physical disability), a special election is available so that dividends could be received and retained by the trust but taxed as if they had been received by the beneficiary, where they would attract little or no tax. The income retained in the trust would then become capital which could be distributed tax-free to a capital beneficiary of the trust, such as the parents. More detailed information about planning for a special needs beneficiary is provided in a separate reference guide, *Planning for a Disabled Beneficiary.*

PRIVACY

Unlike a will, which becomes public once it is probated, a family trust need not be disclosed to anyone other than the parties directly involved. This makes a family trust very useful for a person who wishes to make private arrangements to provide for others.

What are the risks and costs of using a family trust?

In addition to the rules and requirements already mentioned that should be carefully considered when establishing a family trust, there are also some hazards that must be avoided when setting up a family trust. For example:

> In order to avoid a corporate attribution rule, using a family trust in the case of a farm corporation to split income with a spouse is generally recommended only in situations involving corporations whose investment assets (or any assets not used primarily in an active farm in Canada) account for less than 10% of the value of all the corporation's assets.

> If there are a number of different corporations held in the family group, the use of a family trust may inadvertently result in one or more of them being considered to be associated, which could reduce the availability of the lower corporate tax rate for the corporations within the group.

Accordingly, any strategy involving the use of a family trust in the context of a family farm should be made only with the involvement of a professional advisor who is familiar with family trusts and the family's farm interests.

It is also important to be aware of the costs that would be involved in planning and establishing a family trust. For example, there would be professional fees for setting up the trust and drafting the trust document, as well as ongoing costs for matters such as the filing of annual tax returns for the trust and the payment of trustee fees. This should be considered when determining if the use of a family trust would be worthwhile.

Conclusion

In the right circumstances, and with proper planning, a family trust is a useful tool and may provide significant tax savings and other benefits.

Adrian Spitters
FCSI, CFP, FMA
Senior Wealth Advisor

Farm life has always been an important part of my world.

I grew up on a dairy farm on Nicomen Island near Mission, BC and have immediate family and relatives operating dairy, poultry and crop farms.

As co-executor (with two brothers) of my father's estate, I know all too well the result of not having a proper farm transition plan in place.

Our dad had a poorly executed, unworkable Will and a non-existent farm succession plan.

This led to family discord. Despite receiving the majority of the assets, the brother who inherited the farm suffered financial distress and became insolvent. A proper transition plan would have helped him get the financial and farm management training he needed.

Today, I work as a Senior Wealth Advisor with Assante Capital Management Ltd., a leading Canadian wealth management firm, with extensive experience in integrated family farm transitions.

In my work with the *Assante Ag Group*, I provide wealth advisory services to farm and business families. This includes helping them grow, protect and preserve their family assets, wealth and legacy.

In my 30 years in the business, this is what I've seen: that all Canadians, especially farmers, need and want personalized financial advice that helps them achieve their life goals.

It is very clear to me that whether you have a transition plan in place or not, one day you will transfer your farm to your children, extended family or sell to a third party. The question is, will it be on your terms **(voluntarily)**, or someone else's **(involuntarily)**?

Adrian Spitters •
Senior Wealth Advisor •
Assante Capital Management Ltd.
604 - 855 - 6846 •
aspitters@assante.com
Web: www.yourfarmtransitionadvisor.ca

Made in the USA
San Bernardino, CA
26 July 2017